MODERN
POLITICAL
ECONOMY

PRENTICE-HALL FOUNDATIONS OF MODERN POLITICAL SCIENCE SERIES

Robert A. Dahl, Editor

THE AGE OF IDEOLOGY-POLITICAL THOUGHT, 1750 TO THE PRESENT,
Second Edition
by Frederick M. Watkins

THE AMERICAN PARTY SYSTEM AND THE AMERICAN PEOPLE, Second Edition
by Fred I. Greenstein

THE ANALYSIS OF INTERNATIONAL RELATIONS
by Karl W. Deutsch

CONGRESS AND THE PRESIDENCY, Third Edition
by Nelson W. Polsby

DATA ANALYSIS IN POLITICAL SCIENCE
by Edward R. Tufte

MODERN POLITICAL ANALYSIS, Third Edition
by Robert A. Dahl

MODERN POLITICAL ECONOMY
by Norman Frohlich and Joe A. Oppenheimer

NORMATIVE POLITICAL THEORY
by Fred M. Frohock

PERSPECTIVES IN CONSTITUTIONAL LAW, with Revisions
by Charles L. Black, Jr.

THE POLICY-MAKING PROCESS
by Charles E. Lindblom

PUBLIC ADMINISTRATION
by James W. Fesler

PUBLIC OPINION
by Robert E. Lane and David O. Sears

READINGS IN MODERN POLITICAL ANALYSIS, Second Edition
edited by Deane E. Neubauer

READINGS ON STATE AND LOCAL GOVERNMENT
edited by Irwin N. Gertzog

READINGS ON THE INTERNATIONAL POLITICAL SYSTEM
edited by Naomi Rosenbaum

PRENTICE-HALL FOUNDATIONS OF MODERN POLITICAL SCIENCE SERIES

PRENTICE-HALL, INC., Englewood Cliffs, New Jersey 07632

MODERN
POLITICAL
ECONOMY

NORMAN FROHLICH

Management Committee of Cabinet Secretariat
Government of Manitoba

JOE A. OPPENHEIMER

University of Maryland

Library of Congress Cataloging in Publication Data

Frohlich, Norman (date).
  Modern political economy.

  (Prentice-Hall series of foundations of modern
political science)
  Includes bibliographies and index.
  1. Political science. I. Oppenheimer, Joe A.,
joint author. II. Title. III. Series.
JA71.F66   320   77-3379
ISBN 0-13-597120-9

PRENTICE-HALL FOUNDATIONS OF MODERN POLITICAL SCIENCE SERIES

Robert A. Dahl, Editor

MODERN POLITICAL ECONOMY
by Norman Frohlich and Joe A. Oppenheimer

PRENTICE-HALL INTERNATIONAL, INC., London
PRENTICE-HALL OF AUSTRALIA, PTY. LTD., Sydney
PRENTICE-HALL OF CANADA, LTD., Toronto
PRENTICE-HALL OF INDIA PRIVATE LIMITED, New Delhi
PRENTICE-HALL OF JAPAN, INC., Tokyo
PRENTICE-HALL OF SOUTHEAST ASIA PTE. LTD., Singapore
WHITEHALL BOOKS LIMITED, WELLINGTON, New Zealand

10 9 8 7 6 5 4 3 2 1

For Our Children

CONTENTS

PREFACE

Political scientists are continually lamenting the absence of theory in their discipline. Yet surprisingly, one social scientist, Kenneth Arrow, has been awarded a Nobel Prize for his contributions to democratic theory.[1]

Moreover, over the past thirty years, economists and political scientists such as Kenneth Arrow, Duncan Black, Robin Farquharson, John Von Neumann, Oscar Morgenstern, Anthony Down, Mancur Olson, Jr., William Riker, and Gordon Tullock have laid the groundwork for a burgeoning theoretical literature.

The theories that they and others have developed touch upon a wide range of political problems. These theories identify efficient strategies for political organizing, leadership, and coalition formation. Further, they explain voting behavior, bureaucratic phenomena, logrolling, and vote trading. Finally, they present the normative analyses of constitutional democracy and other regimes.

In addition to sharing certain canons of scientific explanation, authors in this area also use psychological assumptions about individual behavior to explain the behavior of groups. More specifically, they all employ similar notions of how individual preferences relate to sets of actions that yield the political behavior of groups and their analyses cover a variety of political contexts.

We hope this book can serve students and professionals seeking an introduction to this literature. The arguments here have been written to be accessible to anyone with a command of simple (high school) algebra, and with a willingness to reason. This has led to a number of pedagogical decisions with which some may disagree. For example, we do not employ such standard means of analyses as indifference curves or calculus in our

---

[1]Arrow was awarded the prize for the corpus of his works, including contributions to general economic theory, but his chief work, *Social Choice and Individual Values,* New Haven: Yale University Press, 1951, deals directly with the problem of democratic constitutions (see Chap. 2 of this volume).

arguments. Moreover, given these objectives, and the growing volume of work in this area, the book cannot be comprehensive. Indeed we have explicitly not dealt with at least one major branch of the findings in this area: those stemming from game theory. This is in part due to the difficulty of incorporating game theory in a book this size. But our decision to omit game theory stemmed also from its adequate treatment in other introductory texts.[2]

Nevertheless, this book should serve as a basis for understanding the rudiments of the field: its methods, assumptions, and principle findings. We hope that for some it will also create a curiosity for further exploration. But for those who wish only to be introduced to these theories, we have tried to present the material in contexts which also furnish the reader some of the excitement of applicability which we felt when first introduced to these works. We have tried to present the theorists' findings and insights into interesting political problems in a spirit that reflects the concerns of the traditional political scientist. Limitations and technicalities of this approach are discussed in the footnotes.

Between the first and last chapters, the book is divided in two. Part I (Chaps. 1–4) is introduced by a presentation of the basic assumptions and their methodological presuppositions. Chap. 1–4 is the application of these assumptions to two types of political phenomena: group decision making (Chap. 1) and organizing (Chaps. 2 to 4). The analysis is designed to be general in that its results can be held to apply in a variety of political regimes and subgroups: totalitarian, bureaucratic, traditional primitive, democratic, etc. The discussion of leadership in Ch. 4 makes some of these applications explicit. Part II (Chap. 5–6) is more narrowly focussed in that it presents theoretical results directly applicable in democratic contexts. Part II's focus, therefore, is on voting and participation in democracies, building democratic coalitions of support and logrolling. The argument can be followed directly in sequence with the chapters.[3]

We have received useful comments and criticism from many sources, but we would particularly like to thank our colleagues, Bill Galston, R. Harrison Wagner, Sam Popkin, and Oran Young for their careful readings of various versions of the manuscript and for their helpful comments. We also owe thanks to our editor, Robert Dahl, for sensitizing us to a number of the normative issues raised by the presentation of this material. But especially we need to thank the numerous students at the University of Texas who suffered through earlier versions of this manuscript, and who by their reactions, gave us incentives to improve the manuscript. Finally we would like to thank each other.

BIBLIOGRAPHIC NOTE

Two elementary treatments of at least part of game theory are available for the mathematically unsophisticated. J. D. Williams, *The Compleat Strategyst,*

---

[2]See the bibliographic note at the end of this preface.

[3]Alternatively, a reader may wish to read Chap. 7 after Chap. 2, or read Chap. 2 after Chap. 6. Such strategies will give more immediate applications of the material in Chap. 2.

New York, McGraw-Hill, 1966 second edition, is a gem of humorous pedagogy. A fuller treatment of two person games can be found in Anatol Rapoport's equally undemanding *Two Person Game Theory: The Essential Ideas,* Ann Arbor: University of Michigan, 1966. More oriented to the political scientist are Steven Brams, *Game Theory and Politics,* New York: Free Press, 1975 and Martin Shubik (editor), *Game Theory and Related Approaches to Social Behavior,* New York: Wiley, 1964, although the latter is somewhat outdated. Three excellent, and more mathematical texts are available for the more serious and industrious scholar.

See Anatol Rapoport's, *N-Person Game Theory: Concepts and Applications,* Ann Arbor: University of Michigan, R. Duncan, 1970; Luce and Howard Raiffa, *Games and Decisions,* New York: Wiley, 1957 (this book also contains a fine discussion of Arrow), and William Riker and Peter Ordeshook's *An Introduction to Positive Political Theory,* Englewood Cliffs, N.J.: Prentice-Hall, 1973 (which covers much of the material in this text as well).

Although no more formal training in mathematics is required from the reader of these three texts than of this volume, the arguments are more symbolized, axiomatized and generalized in those volumes. Correspondingly higher tolerance for mathematical argument is expected of the readers.

letter that Jack Kennedy sent them for signing his nominating petition in 1958.[8]

If O'Brien hadn't thought of this alternative, he could not have chosen it. Thus, to explain choice, one must refer to perceived alternative courses of action.

But choice involves more than the perception of alternatives: it involves the projected consequences of these alternatives. When choosing a course of action, one is also choosing the consequences that he expects to flow from that course of action. Note (again) the importance of perception, or expectation. How often, after a choice, do each of us exclaim, "If I had only known!" Unfortunately, in politics, it is frequently unclear what the consequences of certain courses of action are. For example, Chinese negotiators for Canadian wheat were persuaded to pay interest on loans when the Canadians advised them of a consequence to the Chinese position that the Chinese had not foreseen:

> In one of the discussions that we had on the first long-term agreement in March or April of 1961, the Chinese negotiators pointed out that, according to their reading of the doctrines of Karl Marx, interest was a capitalistic innovation. Therefore, there should not be any interest on these short-term loans of six months. My answer was that I knew that Marx had had a very poor opinion of this matter of interest, but a fundamental principle of Marx was that no good socialist should ever take advantage of workers. I pointed out the sections of Marx's writings to them and indicated that this wheat did not belong to me but to our workers, the farmers. I depicted them getting up at the crack of dawn and going to bed at 10 o'clock at night and emphasized that I did not want to exploit them by having them turn their wheat over to the Chinese and then have to borrow money to live on from the banks, for which they would have to pay 5 percent interest. If the Chinese did not pay that 5 percent, it would be exploitation of the workers for whom I was working.
>
> Then we adjourned. Two days later, they came back and said that I had made a good point. "We will pay 5 percent and an additional one-half per cent," they said, "to make absolutely sure that no one says we are exploiting your workers."[9]

Of course, it may often be that the consequences of an action are uncertain.[10] Here, however, it suffices to note that the perceived consequences of courses of action enter into the determination of choice, even if these consequences are uncertain.

Besides the perception of alternatives and consequences, values or preferences regarding the consequences of the various courses of action are essential to choice. Individuals prefer some states of the world to others.

---

[8]Theodore H. White, *The Making of the President, 1960,* New York: Atheneum, 1961, p. 122.

[9]Alvin Hamilton (former Canadian Minister of Trade and Commerce), in *The United States and China,* edited by Doak Barnett and Edwin O. Reischauer, New York: Praeger, 1970, pp. 128–29.

[10]Much of the discussion in Chap. 3 focuses on choice problems stemming from this fact.

And when we have chosen one over another, our preferences enter into our decision.[11] The notion of preference is so fundamental and familiar that it can be treated as an undefined term in the subsequent analysis. Nevertheless, it is necessary to discuss some characteristics of preference to clarify how preference may be related to the question of choice. We relate these characteristics to choice by using selection rules or choice rules. These rules specify (i.e. predict) an individual's choices as a direct function of his or her preferences regarding the perceived alternative consequences.

III. THE STRUCTURE OF PREFERENCES

Two properties of preference allow us to hypothesize a simple relationship between preference and choice. To identify these properties, let us consider what is commonly meant by the term preference. What does it mean to say "I prefer McGovern to Nixon," or "I prefer Nixon to Wallace?" It would seem that a number of generalizable characteristics underly this use of preference.

Deterministic, or Nonprobabilistic, Preference

To say "I prefer Nixon to Wallace" is quite different from saying "I *probably* prefer Nixon to Wallace." Without the "probably" (or a similar modifier) the statement is quite definite. Inserting "probably" makes it much less definite. The common-sense notion of preference is captured more closely by the former. Ordinary preference is usually viewed as categorical, not probabilistic. In analyzing political-choice behavior, our formulation of preference will conform to the common-sense notion of preference. It will be nonprobabilistic and clear cut. Moreover, we assume that preference is binary: only two things are compared at any one time.[12]

In opting for deterministic preference, we are ignoring certain problems that psychologists have pointed out about human preferences: individuals, at times, give contradictory evidence about their preferences. At one moment a person may say he prefers x to y, later he may say he prefers y to x. Of course we could attribute such apparent contradiction to changes in the choice environment. But some psychologists have attempted a more general approach which describes individuals as having probabilistic preferences. Thus, they assume that " . . . an individual has a certain probability of expressing a preference for one alternative over another."[13] The probabilistic approach poses two problems. First, it does not appear, to us, to be a more realistic representation of actual preference. Second, it would greatly complicate the analysis, and might change some of the major conclu-

[11]This way of stating the problem implicitly assumes that individuals attach values to both the actual course of action undertaken (the means) and the consequences that flow from that course (ends). We assume that individuals evaluate actions and consequences as a whole and decide on that basis. For a similar, yet more formalized account, see William Riker and Peter Ordeshook, *An Introduction to Positive Political Theory*, Englewood Cliffs, N.J.: Prentice-Hall, 1973, pp. 48–53.

[12]See Kenneth J. Arrow, "Rational Choice Functions and Orderings," *Economica*, May 1959 (Vol. 26 n.s.), pp. 121–27 for alternatives to the binary characterization.

[13]Luce and Raiffa, *Games and Decisions*, New York: Wiley, 1957, p. 371. Their first appendix is a relatively accessible (if somewhat dated) treatment of this subject.

sions reached by authors who employed deterministic preference in their analyses. For these reasons we will assume individuals to have determinate preferences.

Preference and Ordering

Consider again the statement "I prefer Nixon to Wallace." It appears to say "No matter how much (or little) I like Wallace, I like Nixon more." Implicit in the statement seems to be a possible order that reflects the individual's ranking of the candidates. Indeed, in common usage preference is understood as a relationship like "heavier than" or "faster than." It relates sets of things by imputing an order to them. In a group of objects we can identify the heaviest, and the next heaviest, and so on. The objects can be ordered according to how much they weigh. Implicit in the everyday usage of preference is a property that allows us to rank alternatives in a similar fashion according to how much they are liked. Since this property plays a major role in subsequent analyses, we will illustrate it by example and discuss it briefly.

Suppose an individual asserts that:

1. he prefers McGovern to Nixon; and
2. he prefers Nixon to Wallace.

The ordinary notion of preference and the formal assumption which we make requires that:

3. he prefers McGovern to Wallace.

More generally, if we write "x is preferred to y," as "xPy," then: if xPy and yPz, it follows that xPz.

This property of preferences is called *transitivity.* If individual preferences are transitive, then all the alternatives can be "well-ordered" whenever there are more than two alternatives. In other words, transitivity allows for the ranking of all alternatives from the most preferred to the least preferred. Consider what happens if transitivity is violated. If we try to rank three football teams when Texas beat Arkansas, Arkansas beat Oklahoma, and Oklahoma beat Texas, we will have trouble deciding which is to be ranked first. Each possible candidate for first is beaten by some other alternative. Which is best? The answer is unclear, for the relationship is intransitive as depicted in Figure I-1. In this case, no ordering yielding a best and a worst team is suggested. No ordering is possible. In order for preferences to generate an ordering, we will want the preferences of the individual to be transitive.[14]

[14]But see Thomas Schwartz, "The Myth of the Maximum," *Nous,* VI, 2 (May 1972), pp. 97–117 for a strong counterargument. One can rule out preference cycles without requiring transitivity. On this, see Amartya K. Sen, *Collective Choice and Social Welfare,* San Francisco: Holden Day, 1970, pp. 15–16, 47–48. Also note that considerable evidence has bee found of *cyclic* preferences. See Kenneth O. May, "Intransitivity, Utility, and the Aggregation of Preference Patterns," *Econometrica,* Jan. 1954 (Vol. 22, No. 1), pp. 1–13, for a preliminary discussion. The unanswered question remains, "What are the precise conditions which generate the individual's preference cycles?"

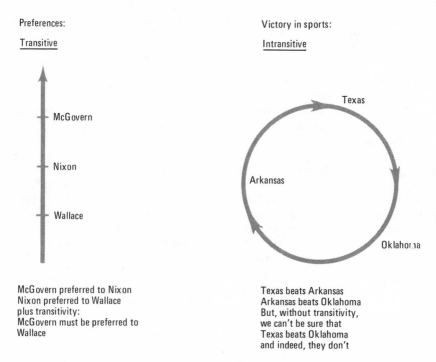

Preferences:

Transitive

McGovern

Nixon

Wallace

McGovern preferred to Nixon
Nixon preferred to Wallace
plus transitivity:
McGovern must be preferred to
Wallace

Victory in sports:

Intransitive

Texas

Arkansas

Oklahoma

Texas beats Arkansas
Arkansas beats Oklahoma
But, without transitivity,
we can't be sure that
Texas beats Oklahoma
and indeed, they don't

Figure I–1   Transitive and intransitive relationships *
*Here "Texas → Oklahoma" should be read as "Oklahoma beats Texas."

But is preference a sufficiently rich concept to allow us to describe fully the structure of an individual's values? Certainly there are times when we can neither say that *x* is preferred to *y* nor that *y* is preferred to *x*. Indeed, we commonly call this situation *indifference:*[15] the relationship that exists in the absence of preference. For convenience, we will assume that indifference is also transitive, although some alternative formulations of indifference leave out this property.[16]

Thus preference, and in its absence, indifference, can be used by the individual to rank alternatives. Given our hypothesis regarding preference, these rankings are "well-behaved." There is always a most preferred alter-

[15]In other words we define indifference between *x* and *y* (*xIy*) in terms of preference (*xPy*) as follows: $xIy = (-xPy \wedge -yPx)$. This definition allows our analysis to be compatible with "indifference curve" techniques, c.f. any standard text on microeconomics for its exposition.

[16]Without transitivity, an individual's indifference between *x* and *y*, and also between *y* and *z*, need not imply his indifference between *x* and *z*. Consider the individual who neither cares whether there are 1,000 or 10,000 U.S. troops in South Korea, nor whether there are 10,000 or 20,000 there. He may find those differences "too small to worry about." But the difference between 1,000 and 20,000 may be sufficiently large to have gone over some "threshold" and he may well prefer having only 1,000 troops there to having 20,000 there. Some psychological theories of perception and choice use these threshold notions in their formulations. See, Sen, *Op. Cit.*, Chap. 1*, for a discussion of the relationship between transitivity of preference and indifference.

izations as "self-interest," they can describe the behavioral consequences of rational choice.

So in the following chapters substantive assumptions about individuals' preferences help generate many of the explanations. Obviously, these statements about generally held values do not reflect our approval of the values. Rather, we chose our premises to be statements which describe and explain political behavior. For example, in Chaps. 3 and 4 we describe most individuals as self-interested and in Chap. 5 we similarly describe politicians. These premises allow the theorist to delineate the consequences of rational action on the part of these individuals but do not signify approval. As Saul Alinsky wrote:

> The fact that we accept working in the world as it is does not in any sense negate, dilute, or vitiate our desires to work toward changing it into the world as we would like it to be.
>
> There is a great difference between the world as it is and the world as we would like it to be. One way to see this quickly is to turn on the television early any evening and watch drama follow drama, in each of which love and virtue always emerge triumphant. This world as we would like it to be continues until the eleven o'clock newscast, when suddenly we are plunged into the world as it is. Here, as you know, love and virtue are not always triumphant. In the world as it is, man moves primarily because of self-interest. In the world as it is, the right things are usually done for the wrong reasons, and vice versa.[24]

With this warning in mind, let us investigate the consequences of the (sometimes nasty) values of individuals for politics. In doing so, we employ the identified characteristics of human choice to open a broad vista of political analysis.

V. FOR FURTHER READING

Readers interested in pursuing further questions associated with scientific explanation and prediction may find that an interesting essay raising some specifically controversial, but basic points is Karl Popper's, "Three Views Concerning Human Knowledge," in *Conjectures and Refutations,* New York: Harper & Row, 1968. A broader, yet equally engrossing and inquiring introduction can be found in Lambert and Brittan's *An Introduction to the Philosophy of Science,* Englewood Cliffs: Prentice-Hall, 1970. Perhaps the most rewarding introduction, and certainly the most controversial (and difficult), can be had from Karl Popper, *The Logic of Scientific Discovery,* New York: Harper and Row, 1965.

Various philosophical schools have been involved in attacking the main pillars upon which the above arguments rest. The reader interested in the better critiques of the above view of science should examine Israel Scheffler, *The Anatomy of Inquiry,* New York: Bobbs Merrill, 1963; Jurgen

---

[24] *Reveille for Radicals,* New York: Random House, 1969, pp. 224–225.

Habermas, *Theory and Practice,* Boston: Beacon Press, 1973; and W. V. O. Quine, *Word and Object,* Cambridge: MIT, 1960.

For those unacquainted with the formal characteristics of logic, there is a fine, almost self-teaching introduction by Robert Jeffrey *Formal Logic: Its Scope and Limits,* N.Y.: McGraw-Hill, 1967. The relationship between logic and mathematics is nicely put in a number of places, but perhaps the deepest introduction to the subject is Ernest Nagel and James R. Newman, *Gödel's Proof,* New York: NYU Press, 1958.

Preference as the underlying element to rationality has been an accepted axiom of microeconomics for more than 2/3 of a century. Certainly, the chapters on consumer choice of any good text of microeconomics could serve as an introduction to the notions and properties of preference and choice. But both Sen, *Collective Choice* (cf. footnote 14) Chaps. 2 and 2* and Kenneth Arrow, *Social Choice and Individual Values,* New Haven: Yale University Press, 1963, Chaps. 1 and 2 are illuminating discussions because they are generalized beyond market choice and hence of particular interest to us.

An alternative formulation of rationality has been developed using the notions of choice set (or maximal set). For illuminating discussions of this, and the forced choice axiom, see Schwartz, "The Myth of the Maximum," (cf. footnote 14) and Arrow, "Rational Choice Functions," (cf. footnote 12). For a view of probabilistic preferences, see Duncan Luce and Howard Raiffa, *Games and Decisions* (cf. footnote 13), appendix 1.

CHAPTER ONE
GROUP CHOICE

Our characterization of rational behavior has been straightforward. Indeed, it is so simple and general, one might not expect it to yield politically relevant predictions. Indeed, if politics were only the choices of single individuals, the analysis would be direct. But, of course, the political-choice situation faced by an individual is within a social context. One does not make such decisions alone. Other people are involved and their preferences generally do not coincide. Moreover, the results of one's choices depend upon how other people make their choices. These two factors vastly complicate the analysis of political decisions. The problems of aggregating many individual preferences and interdependent choices into a group choice lie at the heart of political analysis.

I. RELATING INDIVIDUAL PREFERENCES
TO SOCIAL CHOICES

In common usage, politics involves not only individuals but also groups. Whether we talk about the United States' intervention in Vietnam, the French Revolution, or the signing of the Magna Carta, we are considering choices by numerous individuals that were aggregated to yield a single choice for one or more groups of individuals. If the assumption of individual rational choice is to be of any value in explaining political processes and outcomes, it must enable us to derive consequences about the actions of groups. Thus, some link must be found connecting individual choice and group choice.

Perhaps a group choice or preference consists of the mere sum of the individual choices or preferences. Jean Jacques Rousseau spoke of the "general will" in an ideal participatory democracy as such a "sum." He claims that if "one takes the sum of particular wills . . . (and) . . . take(s) away from these same wills the pluses and minuses that cancel one another . . . the general will remains as the sum of the differences."[1] David Truman spoke about group interests as if they were simply the aggregation of the interests of the constituent members.[2] In these and innumerable other cases, the conclusion is that the group choice can simply be identified by this common or aggregate preference in a manner analogous with the assumptions used for individuals. If groups have transitive preferences, then they can be treated as individuals.

This approach to group choice has considerable intuitive appeal. If it is adopted one can treat the group as a single entity, and talk about group preferences and about group choices. But advantages accrue only if the actions of a group conform to certain rules. If the group is to be treated as a single entity, one requirement is that the group's choices be related to its preferences in a rational manner. But where rational behavior is a relatively simple requirement of individual action, it is a considerably more complex requirement for a group consisting of many individuals. The complexity arises from the identifiable and logically specifiable link between the preference and choice of each of the *individuals* and the preference and choice of the *group* as a summation.

One of the most familiar ways of deriving group choices from the sum of individual preferences is voting.[3] To see the difficulty in getting rational group choice out of rational individual choices using a voting procedure consider the following example of public preferences over American foreign policy during the Vietnam War. In 1967, a public opinion poll on what should be done by the United States in Vietnam was taken.[4] Among the American public responding, the following preferences were voiced: 25 percent wanted a decrease in the level of U.S. involvement, 26 percent wanted the level maintained, and 49 percent wanted the level of involvement increased. For convenience let us refer to the individuals as Standpatters, Doves, and Hawks, respectively. For the sake of this example, let us hypothesize the second and third preferences of the individuals in these groups. Suppose that all the Hawks feel that if the U.S. commitment is not increased so that "victory" can be achieved, then it is better to reduce the commitment than to drag on at the current level of involvement. Thus their preference ranking is higher levels (symbolized by h) are preferred to decreased levels (called d), and decreased levels are preferred to the status quo (hereafter called s). (In Section IV we shall consider what difference it would make if the Hawks had different preferences.) Suppose that all Standpatters feel that if the status quo could not be maintained, they would prefer going to higher levels of involvement to pulling out. Then for them s is preferred to h and h is preferred to d. Finally suppose that the Doves' second choice

[1]Jean Jacques Rousseau, *The Social Contract and Discourse,* Book II, Chap. III, New York: Dutton, 1950, p. 26.

[2]David Truman, *The Governmental Process,* New York: Knopf, 1958.

[3]Of course, this is not the only manner in which preferences can be aggregated. Another method is through market mechanisms.

[4]Such polls are almost beyond counting, the one referred to here has no particularly distinguishing characteristic. See Milton Rosenberg, Sidney Verba, and Philip Converse: *Vietnam and the Silent Majority,* New York: Harper and Row, 1970, p. 31.

is maintenance of the status quo, while their last choice is higher involvement. Symbolically, they prefer d to s and s to h. Then the distribution of preferences can be represented as in Figure 1–1.

Now what if the national policy regarding Vietnam were to be decided by a series of binary or two-way[5] referenda? Any ultimately victorious position in these referenda would be adopted as the group, or social choice. Which alternative would be chosen by the group? What would be the dynamics of the process by which the choice was made?

Arbitrarily, to analyze this situation, let us assume that the first vote is between s and h (see Figure 1–1). In this contest a 51 percent majority (all Standpatters and Doves) prefer s to h. The policy preference of the group is sPh. Now assume that in the second referendum, the vote is between the two policies h and d. A 75 percent majority of the group (Hawks and Standpatters) prefer h to d. Thus the group preference is hPd. Therefore, since the group preference, as expressed by these two majority votes is s over h and h over d, we would expect (and transivity of preferences would require) that s is preferred over d by the group. Let us look at what a vote between s and d would yield. A glance at Figure 1–1 shows that Hawks and Doves, a 74 percent majority, prefer d to s in contrast to our expectations. In other words, majority rule does not yield a transitive preference ordering for the society. Since transitivity is an element of rationality, we note that *in this situation, majority rule does not yield a rational group decision, even though all of the individuals choose rationally.* This is a problem!

The magnitude of the problem cannot be underestimated. *The failure of majority rule to yield transitive preferences in this situation renders any determinate policy choice in such a situation arbitrary.* [6] Were the group's decision procedure to involve political parties, an analogous difficulty could arise. Imagine that the parties only disagree on their Vietnam policy. If one party chose to espouse d while the other party chose s, the social decision would be d over s. If one party had chosen s while the other had espoused h, then s would be the group's choice. D over s and s over h would lead us to expect d over h. But this is *not* the outcome of the contest between d and h. *Therefore, any policy could be adopted and claim majority support in a two-party race.* Clearly, this result is of substantive importance for any evaluation of political results in a democracy. Indeed, such problems have been noted by political observers for some time. This so-called voters' paradox, or cyclical majority problem, has been discussed by Condorcet, Borda, Dodgson, Black and Arrow since the eighteenth century.[7]

---

[5]The assumption regarding binary decision processes is not essential to the analysis at hand and will be dropped.

[6]For example, if the rule specifies that the losers in any contest are to be eliminated, the winner will be determined by the order in which the motions are placed on the agenda.

[7]For an interesting, and yet sophisticated history of the research on the voters' paradox, see Duncan Black's *The Theory of Committees and Elections,* Part II, Cambridge: Cambridge University Press, 1958. More recent works include Kenneth Arrow, *Social Choice and Individual Values,* 2nd ed. New York: Wiley, 1963; Amartya K. Sen, *Collective Choice and Social Welfare,* San Francisco: Holden Day, 1970; David J. Mayston, *The Idea of Social Choice,* New York: St Martins, 1974; and Peter Fishburn, *The Theory of Social Choice* Princeton: Princeton University Press, 1973.

PREFERENCES IN THE GROUP

	HAWKS 49%	STANDPATTERS 26%	DOVES 25%
1st choice	h	s	d
2nd choice	d	h	s
3rd choice	s	d	h

ANALYSIS OF VOTING:

First contest:

Opposing issue positions	s	vs.	h
Opposing voter groups	(doves & standpatters)	vs.	hawks
Vote split (in %).	51%		49%
Outcome	s	beats	h

Second contest:

Opposing issue positions	d	vs.	s
Opposing voter groups	(doves & hawks)	vs.	standpatters
Vote split (in %).	74%		26%
Outcome	d	beats	s

Third contest:

Opposing issue positions	h	vs.	d
Opposing voter groups	(hawks & standpatters)	vs.	doves
Vote split	75%		25%
Outcome	h	beats	d

Diagramatically: (where $x \longrightarrow y$ means "y beats x")

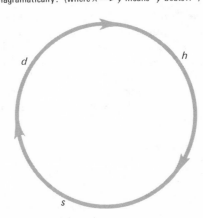

Figure 1–1   Cyclic group choice

The conclusion must be that a majority voting procedure may, at times, be inadquate as a means of generating nonarbitrary group choices from individual preferences. This leads us to the following question: Are there any democratic procedures for reaching group decisions which can lead to transitive, and hence nonarbitrary, group choices? In general, can we base group choice on the preferences of group members in a democratic way and insure that the outcomes are not arbitrary?

II. AN IMPOSSIBILITY THEOREM REGARDING GROUP CHOICE

Kenneth J. Arrow (Nobel Prize, 1972) developed a remarkable proof of the general impossibility of devising a democratic procedure for reaching a group decision that insures transitive,[8] and yet nonarbitrary, group choices. The proof of this impossibility is based on the general assumptions of rational behavior of individuals, and on the specification of a set of five reasonable criteria that might be expected of any democratic procedure generating a group choice from individual preferences. It is assumed that there are at least two individuals in the group and that the decision involves a choice of one from among at least three alternatives. To appreciate the impact of Arrow's result, it is necessary to see what are the five "reasonable" conditions assumed by Arrow.

Nonrestriction of Individual Preferences

The first characteristic that Arrow demands of a democratic decision procedure[9] is that the procedure be able to translate *any* set of individual preferences into a determinate social choice.[10] Such a procedure is analogous to a computer program that translates any set of individual preferences into a group preference. The group-decision procedure must yield a decision for all possible combinations of preferences held by citizens. This may appear to be a reasonable requirement, but some discussion of it is in order.

Some readers may object. After all, doesn't any democratic system require some degree of consensus among the populace if democracy is to work? Thus they reason, that people in a society must share at least a

---

[8]That is, transitive preference *and* indifference.

[9]Arrow's impossibility theorem is of more general concern than our argument suggests. It deals with any procedure that conforms to his conditions—and hence any procedure which links group preferences to the preferences held by the individuals who make up the group. The restriction of the discussion here merely emphasizes the exceptionally strong link of his argument to the analysis of democratic politics. In Chap. 6, a further examination of his argument will extend to the logic of logrolling coalitions and competitions among such coalitions.

[10]The reader who investigates our interpretation of Arrow's conditions may be surprised by some of the substantial differences between their statement in Chap. 3 of Kenneth Arrow, *op. cit.* and in this chapter. Part of the problem is that there have been marginal corrections to the proof over the years. Thus, for example, J.H. Blau, "The Existence of Social Welfare Functions," *Econometrica*, Vol. 25, April 1957, pp. 302–13 pointed to difficulties that required a reformulation of "nonrestriction" and "nonperversity." These are discussed by Arrow in the last chapter of the second edition of his book (cf. pp. 96–103). But there are other difficulties with his formulation and the ensuing literature (especially with regard to the condition of "independence of irrelevant alternatives" as is discussed in fn. 14).

common way of looking at issues. And certainly, many observers of politics believe that the values, and perceptions of individuals within any society have many characteristics in common, stemming from the processes, traditions, and cultural characteristics of the raising and education of children. Such common ground could possibly mean that a democratic group procedure would not have to face all logically possible combinations of individual preference orderings. Rather, it could be, that the preferences held by individuals share characteristics that make it easier to aggregate individual preferences into a group choice. We will discuss some implications of limiting allowable preferences below. For the moment, however, let us assume that a reasonable democratic decision procedure has the property that it can handle *any* set of individual preferences.

Another reasonable objection to Arrow's first requirement would be that a procedure need not result in an entire preference order for a group, but rather need only lead to a choice for the group. That is, a procedure need only specify a choice set from the alternatives considered. Indeed, if we reduce our demands in this manner, Arrow's theorem, as stated below, can *not* be derived. However, now a different impossibility theorem is derivable.[11] Once again the theorem underscores the impossibility of rational choice. So, at this time, we will accept the reasonableness of this condition, noting that one reasonable change will not totally invalidate our results.

Nonperversity or Positive Association

A second characteristic that Arrow specifies for any social choice procedure is that it not translate individual preferences into group choices in a perverse fashion. That is, there must be a positive association between individual values and social choices. Very roughly speaking, this requirement means that the more the individuals value an alternative, the more likely (rather than the less likely) it is to be identified as a social choice by the procedure. Put more technically, if a social-decision procedure yields a group choice in which alternative x is preferred to alternative y (xPy) for a set of individual perferences, then the procedure would yield the same result if the preferences of one or more individuals were modified in x's favor *against y,* and no other changes in preferences occurred.

To see what this condition implies about social choices, let us reexamine our Vietnam example as represented in Figure 1–1. Suppose an acceptable social choice procedure were to yield a social choice of higher levels of U.S. involvement as opposed to a maintenance of the status quo in Vietnam under the preferences of the individuals. Then the condition of positive association would require that the same procedure yield the same choice of higher involvement over the status quo if the Doves were to change their preferences between those two alternatives in favor of higher involvement. Clearly, any decision procedure that did not yield this result would be perverse and unacceptable. It would "demote" alternatives as they became more popular. The condition is therefore reasonable and desirable.

[11]Sen, *op. cit.,* p. 55, Theorem 4*5 and his discussion of the theorem on p. 50–51.

Independence of Irrelevant Alternatives[12]

A third condition that Arrow requires of a social-choice procedure is the so-called *independence of irrelevant alternatives*. A group's choice of a particular alternative from a set of alternatives should not depend upon alternatives from which they are not to make a selection. Or, as Arrow put it:

> [T]he choice made from any fixed environment S should be independent of the very existence of alternatives outside of S . . . if we consider two sets of individual orderings such that, for each individual, his ordering of those particular alternatives in a given environment is the same each time, then we require that the choice made by society from that environment be the same when individual values are given by the first set of orderings as when given by the [identical] second.[13]

Given that we have also assumed transitivity of the social preference ordering, one consequence of this condition can be immediately stated. If we are faced with how the group is to order a pair of alternatives, it is sufficient to know the rankings of this pair by each individual in the group. It is instructive to see just why this is the case. The independence of irrelevant alternatives insures that the rules for group choice do not allow the choice set of S (i.e. $C(S)$) to change if neither S, nor the individual preferences over S, change. In other words, independence of irrelevant alternatives insures us that the group's choice from a pair of alternatives only depends upon the identification of the alternatives and the preferences regarding *those two* alternatives. This implication can now be combined with the conclusion mentioned on pages 11–12. The conjunction of forced choice and transitivity insure that if we know the choice sets from all pairwise comparisons of alternatives in S, we could construct the preference ordering over S. Hence, the preferences of the individuals over any two alternatives determine the choice set of those alternatives (by independence) and these choice sets are all that are needed to establish the social ranking of these alternatives (by forced choice and transitivity).[14] As Sen has put it:

---

[12]We are deeply indebted to Jeff Richelson who pointed out an error in earlier drafts of this volume regarding our formulations in this section. His patience and quality as a teacher is hopefully reflected in what is clearly an improved discussion for all readers.

[13]Arrow, *op. cit.* 26–27.

[14]Usually readers are not shown the need to use transitivity in conjunction with the independence of irrelevant alternatives (IIA) in the derivation of this result. Thus, it has often been falsely claimed that IIA alone leads to the "separability" of preferences. At times this has led to confusion of otherwise clear-headed personages. So when Plott commented on Arrow's use of the example of rank-order voting not fulfilling IIA (cf. Arrow, p. 27), Plott was right. But given that rank-order voting was a "social decision rule" and thus had to conform to Axioms I & II in Arrow, (transitivity, connexity) Arrow was right in arguing that it did not conform to IIA. In any case Plott's paper ["Rationality and Relevance in Social Choice Theory," Social Science Working Paper, Number 5, California Institute of Technology, Pasadena, August 1971] led to a number of other comments on other usages. So for example, see Steven J. Brams, *Paradoxes in Politics*, Free Press, 1976, p. 35–36, who criticizes others for alternative formulations of IIA which allow for the more direct observation of the result of "separability." If the argument here is correct, these definitions of IIA may be more stringent than needed, but are not deleterious if we consider only social rules which guarantee transitive results. Of course they are overstated restrictions on the conditions and hence also "undersell" Arrow results.

Suppose the choice is between x and y, and individual rankings of x and y remain the same, but the rankings of x vis-a-vis another alternative z changes, or the rankings of z vis-a-vis another alternative w alters. What is required is that the social choice between x and y should remain the same.[15]

An illustration of the contents of this condition can be seen within the context of our example regarding U.S. policy in Vietnam. Suppose that a social choice procedure were to yield a ranking of increased involvement over the status quo when the contest involved only these two alternatives. If everyone's preferences stayed the same, independence of irrelevant alternatives implies that the existence of a third possibility (e.g. decreased involvement), which was not even to be voted upon would not affect the outcome of the vote.

On the surface, this condition appears quite reasonable. At a minimum, it is difficult to construct a *prima facia* case against it. For the moment, we will suspend discussion of this condition and accept it as a reasonable requirement of a social choice procedure. But we will discuss some characteristics of group-choice procedures that do not conform to this condition, below. This discussion will, we think, further reinforce the reasonableness and desirability of this condition in any democratic social choice procedure.

Citizens' Sovereignty

A fourth condition required of a reasonable social-choice procedure is the condition of citizens' sovereignty, or nonimposition. Put simply, this condition stipulates that some pattern of preferences of the group members is sufficient for the adoption of each alternative. In other words, each alternative is a logically possible choice for the group, and it is chosen if the appropriate pattern of preferences prevails in the group.

Many groups do not have citizens' sovereignty. For example, American schools have student councils, but these councils cannot decide to change the grading techniques no matter how they vote. But the lack of sovereignty of student councils goes without saying and is in obvious juxtaposition with the sovereignty of the citizenry as a whole. A lack of sovereignty would mean that a social decision could be imposed upon the whole group without any regard to the preferences of the individuals who made up the group. Such a possibility clearly violates the spirit of democracy. So we insist, along with Arrow, that for every pair of alternatives (x and y) there is some possible set of preferences of the group members that yields a group choice of x over y.

Nondictatorship

The final condition required of an acceptable democratic social-choice procedure is that it cannot allow any single individual to be a dictator. Put another way, there cannot be any individual who can determine the groups' rankings between every pair of alternatives regardless of the preferences of others. No one can get his or her own way under all conceivable circumstances.

[15]Sen, *op. cit.*, p. 37.

Each of these conditions taken individually seems to embody a property that would be considered desirable in a democratic constitution, or group-choice procedure. In developing a procedure for reaching group choices from individual preferences, it might appear reasonable to ask that the procedure conform to these five criteria, and that it insure transitive choices. It is Arrow's remarkable result that *it is impossible to find a decision procedure that conforms to these five criteria and insures transitive group decisions.* The five conditions specified earlier are logically inconsistent with transitive group choice. They cannot all be satisfied simultaneously! Put another way, *any group-decision procedure that conforms to the first three conditions and insures transitivity of choice, leads to decisions that are either imposed or dictatorial.*

III. OVERVIEW AND PROOF
OF ARROW'S IMPOSSIBILITY THEOREM*

To appreciate the power and elegance of the argument, we will informally sketch a proof of Arrow's theorem. The proof consists of showing that if a social choice procedure conforms to conditions 1–4, and yields transitive results, then there must be a dictator! In other words, the proof will be by contradiction. We will assume that we have a decision procedure that satisfies the first four conditions and that insures transitive group choice. We then need only examine the necessary logical characteristics of any such procedure. Such examination leads to the conclusion that any such procedure must violate the last condition. That is, if we assume the procedure conforms to the first four conditions and transitivity, it follows that the procedure must be dictatorial. We begin the proof by defining some terms that will enable us to draw out some implications of the decision procedure's characteristics.

Note that given nonperversity and citizens' sovereignty, when all the individuals in the group unanimously prefer x to y, the society must prefer x to y. In other words, the group, when unanimous, is always a "decisive set."[16] Indeed, this notion of a decisive set can be generalized. We define a set of individuals, V, as decisive for alternative x against y (i.e. $D_V(x,y)$),[17]

---

*Although simplified, this section may still prove too technical for some readers. The reader can proceed to section IV if he or she begins to bog down in the proof.

[16]To prove this, consider any two alternatives x and y and any set of individual preferences A* in which all individuals prefer x to y. If we can show that xPy for A*, we have shown that the set of all individuals is decisive. From citizens' sovereignty we know that there is *some* set of individual preferences, call it A, which yields a social choice xPy. Consider the following set of preferences A' derived from A. In each individual's ranking of preferences in A, move x to the most preferred position; A' is now like A, except that in A' each individual ranks x as most preferred. But we know that for the set of preferences, A, xPy. By the condition of positive association, the social choice of xPy is preserved when x has been raised in everyone's preferences. Therefore, for A', xPy. Notice in the set of preferences A', all individuals prefer x to y. Now A' can be modified by shifting the rankings of all alternatives other than x and y to achieve A*. By transitivity plus independence of irrelevant alternatives, shifting the rankings of alternatives other than x and y in moving from A' to A* does not affect the social choice between x and y. Since for A' xPy, then for A* xPy. Therefore, the social choice for the set of rankings A* is xPy and the set of all individuals is decisive for x against y.

[17]The notation here stems from Sen, *op. cit.*, pp. 42–43.

if when all the individuals in V prefer x to y and all other individuals prefer y to x, the social choice is x over y. Remember that the group as a whole is always a decisive set, i.e. it's decisive for any pair of alternatives, and hence, there must be, for every pair of alternatives, some decisive set. Furthermore, it is easy to see that if V can get its way when everyone opposes it, then, by nonperversity, it must be the case that V can always get its way on the choice between that pair of alternatives for which it is decisive.

We can now prove Arrow's theorem. First, we will show that the smallest decisive set will consist of only one individual. Then we will demonstrate that if *one* individual is decisive for some pair of alternatives, under a rule conforming to the specified conditions, he must be decisive for *every* pair of alternatives, and hence is a dictator.

To begin, let us consider the smallest decisive set. Define a *minimal decisive set* as a set of individuals which is decisive for some x against some y, and which contains no proper subset that is decisive for *any* alternative against any other alternative. At least one such (nonempty) set must exist for some pair of alternatives, since the set of all individuals is decisive for any x against any y, and the empty set (i.e. the set with no individual members) is not decisive for any x against any y.[18] Thus, some decisive set must be a minimal decisive set. Given that the rules for social choice must conform to the first four conditions specified above, what must be the size of such a minimal decisive set? How many individuals does it take to be "decisive" given Arrow's conditions?

Let V be a minimal decisive set for some pair of alternatives, a and b, which we can write as $D_V(a,b)$. Let j be one individual in V and let W be the set of all other individuals in V.[19] This makes W a proper subset of V and thus W cannot be decisive. V *could* be composed of only one individual j, which would require W to be empty. Let U be all individuals not in V. Finally, let y be an alternative different from a and b.

Assume the following preferences:

1. All individuals in V prefer a to b. One person in V (called j), prefers b to y, as do all members of the group outside of V (i.e. in U).
2. All individuals outside of V (i.e. in U) also prefer b to a. Or:

	V		U
	(j)	W	
more preferred	a	[no individuals necessarily	b b
	b	in W, but if anyone is in	and
less preferred	y	in W, they prefer a to b]	y a

[18]Note that this definition is not the same as has traditionally been used.
[19]In set theoretic terms: $\{j\} \cup W = V$, $\{j\} \cap W = \phi$.

Since V is assumed to be decisive for a against b, and all individuals in V are assumed to prefer a to b, the group's decision must be aPb. Furthermore, all individuals in U, plus one (i.e j), prefer b to y. Thus, only individuals in W could prefer y to b. Since V was assumed to be a minimal decisive set, W (a proper subset of V) cannot be decisive. Thus, regardless of whether anyone is in W, and regardless of the preferences of any individuals who may be in W, the social choice cannot be yPb. For if yPb for the group, when all individuals outside of W prefer b to y, W would have to be decisive for b against y, and V would not conform to the definition of a minimal decisive set.

Thus, the group choice must be either bPy or bIy (indifference between b and y). In either case, it can now be shown that the group must choose a over y: aPy. For given aPb (because V is decisive) and not yPb (because V is minimal decisive, and W is a proper subset of V), aPy. After all, if either aPb and bPy, or aPb and bIy then, *by transitivity alone*, aPy. Thus, without further stipulation of preferences (for any possible members of W) it is clear that aPy, even though j and conceivably j alone, would support such a social choice. In other words, j appears to be a decisive set for a versus y because if he prefers a to y when all others are opposed, society's preferences are those of j. But what is this? Have we not merely shown that j is a minimum decisive set for a given a against any y given a stipulated set of preferences (i.e. for all i not in W, bP_iy)? No. We can easily generalize the conclusion. Remember: the rules by which social choices are made cannot violate independence of irrelevant alternatives. Thus, it follows that *if* there is a set of preferences such that when j alone prefers a to y, (and all others prefer y to a) so *must* society. Then the introduction of other preferences, over *other* pairs of alternatives, must not affect the social choice between a and y alone. Indeed, this was the thrust of the argument made when independence of irrelevant alternatives was introduced (see page 21). Thus, when V is defined as a minimal decisive set for a versus b, we see that it has to contain another decisive set, j. But this violates the definition of minimal decisive set (that no proper subset of minimal decisive set also be a decisive set) unless $V = j$.

Thus, whenever V is a minimal decisive set for some pair of alternatives (a,b), $V = j$ and:

1. if $D_V(a,b)$ then $D_j(a,b)$ and we also showed,
2. if $D_j(a,b)$ then $D_j(a,y)$.

So if the rule conforms to the first four conditions Arrow specified, the minimal decisive set must be a single individual! How much power must that individual have? We have already seen [in (2) above] that if the individual is decisive for a specified pair (a,b) of alternatives, he is decisive for one element of that pair against all comers (a,y). But does j have still more power? We can now generalize our findings to show that j can control the social choice for *any* pair of alternatives: $Dj(x,y)$, and hence j is a dictator.

We do this by showing that j is decisive for any x against any y, different from a, and then that j is decisive for any x against a. To show that j is decisive for any x against any y, different from a, consider the following set of preferences:[20]

	j	U
more preferred:	x	y
$\uparrow$	a	x
less preferred:	y	a

Since all prefer x to a, xPa. We already know j is decisive for a against y: hence aPy. Thus, xPa and aPy, which, by transitivity requires that xPy. But only j prefers x to y. Therefore, j is decisive for x against y, where $y \neq a$.

We now show that j is decisive for x against a. Since j is decisive for x against any $y \neq a$, we will have shown that j is decisive for any x against any other alternative. To do this consider the following set of preferences.

	j	U
more preferred:	x	y
$\uparrow$	y	a
less preferred:	a	x

Since j is decisive for x against y, xPy. Since all individuals prefer y to a, yPa. Therefore, transitivity yields xPa. But since j is the only individual who prefers x to a, j must be decisive for x against a. Thus, the set consisting of j must be decisive for any x against any y. Put in common language, j gets his way in all cases for any x against any y in which all others in the group oppose his preferences. This being true, the conditions of positive association and of independence of irrelevant alternatives indicates that j *always gets his way*. If others were to change their preference rankings of x against y in y's favor or to change their rankings of other alternatives, the result xPy would stand. Thus j *is a dictator* in all cases. Or, when V designates a minimal decisive set:

3. If $D_{I'}(a,b)$ then $(V = j)$ then $D_j(a,b)$ then $D_j(a,y)$ and then $D_j(x,y)$.

---

[20]At this point the reader may wish to protest: "You can't alter the preferences for this would change the situation. Wasn't the proof that j was decisive contingent upon the set of preferences postulated?" Not quite, for recall that the assumptions of independence of irrelevant alternatives and transitivity imply that if the preferences of a relative to y are not changed, then the outcome cannot change. Hence, the relevant question is: "Have we changed the preferences of j or the members of U with respect to the pair a,y?" The answer is no, and hence must still be decisive for the pair a,y.

But remember we assumed the first four conditions of Arrow, plus transitivity, and then showed that these assumptions implied that there existed "minimal decisive sets." Further, we showed that such a set, which given the conditions must exist, must contain only one individual. From there, we proceeded to show that the single individual who makes up the minimum decisive set could get his (or her) way on all issues, regardless of the preferences of others. This individual is a dictator. But the fifth condition is that there is no dictator. To satisfy the first four conditions, plus transitivity, there must be a dictator and thus, the five conditions plus transitivity are inconsistent. *It is logically impossible for there to be a social-choice procedure that satisfies all the conditions.*

Sometimes the logical steps of a proof do not serve to indicate in an intuitively understandable manner "why" the outcome has been reached. That is, if the conclusions follow deductively, they are (in some sense) contained in the premises. The "alert reader" may feel that he or she should not be "surprised" when the conclusion is reached. For this reason it is worth considering why the outcome should *not* be "surprising," given the premises. Much of the argument comes from the juxtaposition of transitivity with the requirement for independence of irrelevant alternatives. Thus, Arrow's transitivity requirement allows us to derive, from xPy and yPz, that xPz. In this derivation, y plays an important (and not independent) function. However, independence of irrelevant alternatives must allow us to assert that if xPz, it must be true regardless of how people feel about y. Obviously transitivity and independence are potentially at odds, given carefully constructed situations. And it is precisely the tension between these two normatively desirable characteristics of decision rules that Arrow uses to advantage in his proof.

IV. GROUP CHOICE PROCEDURES RE-EXAMINED

The implications of this impossibility theorem are wide ranging. It is difficult to overstate the theory's importance in the evaluation of democracy. If the five conditions reflect the norms that underlie democratic government, then we must face the conclusion that transitivity is sacrificed in democratic governments and examine the implications of that sacrifice. Giving up transitivity leads either to endless cycling and indecision, or to arbitrary choices. Since even democratic governments must make choices, the results must be arbitrary.

The possibility of intransitive social choices means that the order in which issues are put to a vote determines which alternative will be adopted. In any cyclical majority situation (where losers are eliminated), any alternative can get a majority if put to a vote at the appropriate time. Thus, control of the agenda in a cyclical majority situation is tantamount to dictatorial power.

Thus, in an evaluation of a democratic system, we may well focus our attention on the control of agendas, and on whether there are any groups with a monopoly of such control. Are all the agendas controlled in the same manner by the same groups? What difference does this make? Such questions will be raised again when we look at the coalition formation process. But now they contradict the everyday homily that democratic decisions represent the will of the people. The relevant questions raised by democracy may not be who votes, but who decides on how the voting is to take place.

On the other hand, the criticism may be too harsh. After all, we may agree with some of the more obvious requirements of Arrow, but perhaps some of the conditions are unnecessary. Nondictatorship, nonimposition, and nonperversity seem beyond question. But what of unrestricted preferences and independence of irrelevant alternatives?

Restricting Preferences

It may be that the preferences of individuals may be restricted without doing violence to the ethical claims of democracy. Certainly, not requiring the first condition would increase the chances of avoiding the paradoxical and unpalatable conclusions of Arrow. Let us examine some sorts of restrictions on preferences and follow some of the implications of these restrictions on the possibility for democracy.

Consider again the cyclical majority situation regarding a choice of policies *vis-a-vis* Vietnam. The cycle in that case stemmed from a particular pattern of individual preferences. The preferences for Doves (in descending order) were d, s, h; for Standpatters s, h, d; and for Hawks h, d, s. If the individuals in question shared a particular way of evaluating the underlying issue involved in their ranking of alternatives, it can be shown that the stated set of preferences could not emerge, and a cyclical majority situation would not be possible. For example, let the individuals agree that the three alternatives can be placed along a line representing "degree of involvement." Further let each individual be able to identify his first preference as a point on that line. (Figure 1–2 represents one such continuum.) If each individual prefers points closer to his preferred points over points further away, then individuals may be said to have *single peaked preferences*.[21] For most people, an everyday example of a single peaked preference is the amount of sugar in coffee. Thus, each individual has a personal "ideal" amount of sugar in a cup of coffee. The more the actual amount departs from the ideal, presumably, the worse the coffee tastes. If the preferences are restricted in this fashion, the possibility of cyclical majorities disappears. In this particular example, the restriction of possible preference orderings results in a switch of the second and third preferences of the Hawks from dPs to sPd. The result as indicated in Figure 1–2 is an unequivocal victory for the status quo policy.

If we had reason to believe that in a given society single peaked preferences on *each* issue were the rule, then we might hope that the social choice

---

[21]This is, in fact, a somewhat more restrictive definition of single peaked preferences than is necessary. For a full discussion of voting, when preferences are single peaked, see Black, *op. cit.*, Part I. Also see William H. Riker and Peter C. Ordeshook, *An Introduction to Positive Political Theory*, Englewood Cliffs, N.J.: Prentice-Hall, 1973, pp. 100–109; or R. Duncan Luce and Howard Raiffa, *Games and Decisions: Introduction and Critical Survey*, New York: Wiley, 1957, pp. 353–357. The best analysis of the precise conditions required to remove cycles can be found in Sen, *op. cit.*, pp. 166–171 and Chap. 10*. For a fuller discussion on the nature of the single-peakedness assumptions, see Chap. 6 of this volume.

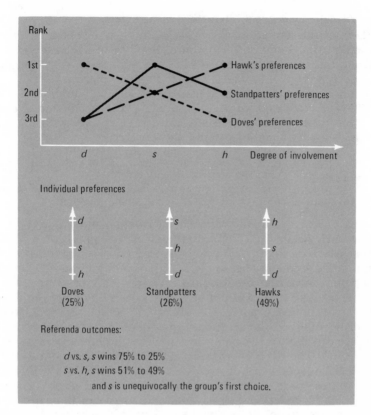

Figure 1–2   Social choice with common evaluative basis of the issue

identified as the voter's paradox might never occur. Unfortunately, unless *all* issues are decided *one at a time* and are never aggregated into a program, the possibility of a cyclical majority problem exists even if preferences are single peaked on each issue.[22] In any society, the conditions necessary for all citizens to have single peaked preferences on each issue are likely to be restrictive indeed. Such a society is likely to be rare. Moreover, there is likely to be a degree of arbitrariness in the determination of which preference orderings are to be ruled out if Arrow's first condition is violated. Who determines what preference orderings are to be ruled out? How are they ruled out? Sacrificing Arrow's first condition raises many additional questions about the arbitrariness of social decisions and does not, in general, resolve the cyclical majority problem in any case.

[22]To see how combining issues can change things, see Chapter 7 on coalitions. Also the more mathematically inclined reader may wish to examine Tullock, *Toward a Mathematics of Politics,* Ann Arbor: University of Michigan Press, 1968, Chapters 3 and 4, Duncan Black and R.A. Newing, *Committee Decisions with Complementary Valuations,* London: Hodge, 1951, and Joseph B. Kadane, "On Division of the Question" *Public Choice,* Vol. XIII, Fall 1972, pp. 47–55.

Allowing Independent Alternatives to be Relevant

Another possible alteration of Arrow's result might be obtained if one chose to abandon the condition of the independence of irrelevant alternatives. However, this sacrifice, too, introduces a new element of arbitrariness into social decisions.

Consider the election of a leader in a simple plurality system. Each voter has one vote, and whichever candidate receives the most votes wins. Now what happens in a three way race for the leadership in which the individuals are assumed to vote for their preferred candidate:

a. 35 percent prefer the incumbent leader, i, to the other two contestants.
b. 40 percent prefer the main opponent, m.
c. 25 percent prefer the secondary opponent, s. Their second choice is the incumbent, and their last choice is the main opponent.

If a vote were held, the social choice would be the election of the main opponent. He would get a plurality (40 percent to 35 percent to 25 percent). In other words, m would beat i. But suppose an assassination attempt were to cripple the secondary opponent and remove him from the contest prior to the vote. Then, if a vote were held, the ordering of m and i would not be the same. The winner would not be the main opponent but the incumbent. The incumbent would get the votes of his supporters and of those who previously voted for the secondary opponent. Thus, the removal of one candidate can affect the social ordering of two others. The result would be iPm, not mPi. This decision procedure, therefore, violates one of the consequences of independence of irrelevant alternatives plus transitivity.[23]

In other words, getting rid of the requirement that the social-decision rule obey independence of irrelevant alternatives can allow the ranking of two alternatives to be affected by the ranking of other alternatives. But this indicates how the abandonment of the independence of irrelevant alternatives introduces another element of arbitrariness into the decision procedure. For if $C([x,y])$ is not determined solely by the preferences of the individuals over $[x,y]$, then the strategic introduction of other alternatives can be used to thwart the original choice. Thus, the possibility of running "stalking horses" to "divide and conquer" and wreak havoc among one's opponents becomes the standard way for the democratic decision to be manipulated. In other words, when independence isn't required, the alternative can be manipulated by the strategic introduction or removal of alternatives for consideration in the contest. Control of which alternatives are to be considered under such a procedure can result in control of which alternative is chosen. Relaxation of the condition that social choices be independent of irrelevant alternatives leads to but another form of arbitrariness.

Any further attempts to avoid the arbitrariness of social decisions implied by Arrow's theorem would require a rejection of one of the three

---

[23]See, once again, pp. 21–22 of this chapter. One shouldn't be surprised that such a "common" rule as plurality violates one of the conditions; *every rule must* violate at least one of them according to the proof.

remaining conditions. But these are so fundamental that their rejections are tantamount to the abandonment of a basic democratic ideal. Any decision procedure that perversely relates individual preferences to social choices, or is imposed, or is dictatorial, is not acceptable. We must be prepared to face up to the conclusions of Arrow's demonstration.

Architects of the good democracy, beware. There is more than a little of the arbitrary in any political process. Voting rules, no matter how faithfully executed and enforced, by themselves cannot lead to intuitively justifiable decisions. Problems regarding agenda, strategy, and leadership clearly loom large in the process.

Our simple definition of individual rational choice and the conclusion that political situations require group choices has led us to a paradox. We have seen the impossibility of constructing reasonable democratic procedures for reaching group choices from individual preferences. But, of course, group choices lie at the heart of political activity. If we are to explain political behavior we must go beyond Arrow's interesting, but still negative, result.

To see what else can be said about group activities in politics, we turn our attention to group actions in the absence of explicit rules for generating group choices. The assumption of individual rationality in those cases will lead to further counter-intuitive and politically relevant results.

V. FOR FURTHER READING

Various alternative elementary presentations of Arrow's theorem are available. But the serious student is well advised to begin by going to Arrow's *Social Choice and Individual Values* (cf. footnote 7), as many of the chapters contain discursive and well rounded discussions of the major points which have later been subject to scrutiny. For a clear presentation of the proof, with a different pedagogical emphasis, see Chapter 14, Howard Luce and Duncan Raiffa, *Games and Decisions* (cf. footnote 20). A.K. Sen, *Collective Choice and Social Welfare* (cf. footnote 7) also presents Arrow's results but goes far beyond to deal with related important topics. His presentation is aimed (successfully) at both mathematically sophisticated and unsophisticated students. Jeffrey Richelson presents a clear overview and analysis of the alternative restrictions which can be placed on social choice functions in "Conditions on Social Choice Functions," *Public Choice*, XXVII (Winter, 1976). On the other hand, only for the mathematically adept are the extremely technical presentations of important extensions of Arrow's work in Peter Fishburn, *The Theory of Social Choice* (cf. footnote 7).

On single peaked preferences, the seminal work is Duncan Black's *The Theory of Committee and Elections* (cf. footnote 20) and Black and Newing, *Committee Decisions with Complementary Valuation* (cf. footnote 21). Finally, an excellent review of the implications of these arguments for democratic theory (and one that presupposes no mathematical abilities) is Charles R. Plott, "Axiomatic Social Choice Theory: An Overview and Interpretation," *American Journal of Political Science*, XX, August 1976, No. 3, pp. 511–96.

CHAPTER TWO

COLLECTIVE ACTION
IN UNORGANIZED
GROUPS

"Rational choice" for an individual requires transitive preferences and the selection of the most preferred alternative. Although we raised no major objection to the assumption that *individuals* choose rationally, we have shown that there are reasons to doubt that *groups* of rational individuals can choose rationally. The voters' paradox and Arrow's impossibility theorem demonstrate that in using voting procedures, groups can violate the transitive preference characteristic of rational behavior.[1]

But the barriers to rational group action do not end with intransitivities in voting. The second characteristic of rationality, the choice of the most preferred alternative (or optimization), is also, in general, violated in group choices. That is, in pursuing common interests, groups of individuals characteristically do not choose the optimal alternative. To see why this is so, we will again examine some typical objectives of political action on the part of rational individuals and derive consequences for the behavior of groups of individuals. Doing this will put the lack of optimizing behavior in proper perspective.

I. THE OBJECTIVES OF POLITICAL ACTION:
COLLECTIVE GOODS

Cleaning up the environment, ending inflation, establishing a more equitable political system through a revolution, and winning an election are quite typical political objectives. Not only are these typical political goals, but attaining them requires that individuals engage in political actions. These objectives have another common characteristic: the securing (or nonsecuring) of these objectives will be shared by all members of a group. Consequently, these and similar phenomena can be analyzed in terms of collective

---

[1]There is nothing in Arrow's argument to restrict it to such a narrow interpretation. Indeed, he himself extends his results beyond the simple analysis of voting in Chaps. 4 and 7.

goods: goods[2] which if consumed by one member of a specified group, cannot be withheld from the other members. Indeed, much of politics is concerned with the securing (or nonsecuring) of collective goods. The reason for this is well expressed by Mancur Olson:

> *The achievement of any common goal or the satisfaction of any common interest means that a public or collective good has been provided for that group.* The very fact that a goal or purpose is common to a group means that no one in the group is excluded from the benefit or satisfaction brought about by its achievement.
>
> . . . It is of the essence of an organization that it provides an inseparable, generalized benefit. It follows that the provision of public or collective goods is the fundamental function of organizations generally. A state is first of all an organization that provides public goods for its members, the citizens; and other types of organizations similarly provide collective goods for their members (italics in original).[3]

Therefore, to analyze the political choices of groups, we must conside how groups of rational individuals supply themselves with collective goo s.

First, we will identify the characteristic ways in which other goo ls are supplied. The distinctive characteristics of "private goods" can be illustrated by reference to a case of Coca Cola. It will immediately be seen that in a market economy the problems of obtaining this sort of good are different from the problems involved in securing a collective good.

A case of Coke is *divisible:* each individual who consumes a bottle gets his own. The bottles of Coke can be *divided up* among consumers. Thus, the amount that any group of individuals might consume is equal to the *sum* of their shares. Furthermore, it is possible to give a bottle to one individual in a group and withhold it from another. Each individual can be *excluded* from consumption. We refer to this characteristic of the good as *excludability.* In general, excludability and divisibility have been used as the defining characteristics of private goods.

Economists have used these two characteristics of private goods, and the assumption of rational behavior, to develop explanations of the supply and demand of private goods in a market. In a market, the consumer must pay a price to get a good (i.e., not to be excluded from it). When the

---

[2]"Goods" will be used here in the "economic" sense: as a combination of scarce sources. The word is not meant to connote positive valuation. A "good" may not be good. Indeed, "goods" may have negative valuations placed upon them. Thus some individuals might be willing to pay to get rid of some "goods" (e.g., pollution). Similarly, "benefits" should not be viewed as necessarily carrying a positive valuation. One of the "benefits" of residing on the eastern coast of the United States is the breathing of industrial wastes.

[3]Mancur Olson, Jr., *The Logic of Collective Action,* Cambridge: Harvard University Press, 1965, p. 15. The original analysis of this problem goes back many years. But more modern analytic work that served as a foundation for Olson and others began with Paul Samuelson, "The Pure Theory of Public Expenditure," *Review of Economics and Statistics,* XXXVI, Nov. 1954, pp. 347–49, 387, 389. Other contributions include Julius Margolis, "A Comment on the Pure Theory of Public Expenditure," *Ibid,* Nov. 1955, pp. 347–49. Another branch of literature that is closely related is found in the discussions of externalities, or economic effects, for which the market does not properly compensate. A good collection of articles on this subject has been edited by Robert Staaf and Francis Tannian, *Externalities,* New York: Dunnellen, 1972.

consumer pays the price, he gets a unit of the good, thereby simultaneously excluding others from the consumption of that particular unit of the good. Indeed, in a market economy, individuals pay the price to get what they want *precisely because of excludability:* if they don't pay, they are excluded from consumption. Similarly, divisibility has direct consequences when coupled with excludability. For example, the more consumers to be satisfied in the market (i.e., to receive units of the good), the larger must be the quantity of the good supplied. The interaction between a set of profit-seeking producers and a set of rational consumers regarding private goods is precisely the subject matter of market economics.[4]

How different are the properties of collective goods! Collective goods are nonexcludable. This means that individuals cannot each be charged a price for consumption. By definition, if any one individual in a group were to get a collective good, all the individuals would get it. Moreover, collective goods are not divisible. Whereas providing an increasing number of individuals with Coke requires the production of more bottles of Coke, one collective good, such as a stop-light, suffices even if the traffic at an intersection increases. Reducing the level of pollutants in the air of a major city is a collective good that demonstrates the nonexcludability and indivisibility of such goods. If the air is clean, everyone benefits. People cannot be excluded from the clean air because they have not paid for its procurement. It is nonexcludable. Moreover, if the air is cleaned, any number of individuals can breathe the pure air. No additional production of clean air is needed to supply new air to each new breather; the clean air is indivisible.

Since, by definition, collective goods are not divisible and do not support exclusion, the analysis of a pricing mechanism and a market cannot be used directly to analyze the supply and demand of such goods. The market explanation developed for "private goods" cannot be employed directly to explain how groups provide themselves with collective goods.

Thus, the stuff of politics. Interests held in common by a number of individuals can be looked at in terms of collective goods. What is to be gained by this "shift in terminology"? After all, in the immortal words of Gertrude Stein, "A rose is a rose is a rose." What can we expect to gain by the translation of political problems into problems involving the demand and supply of collective goods?

Perhaps we should begin with some things we *cannot* conclude from the public versus private good distinction. We certainly cannot conclude the need for a relationship between public versus private ownership and collective versus private goods. Obviously, public ownership or socialism is consistent with market economies. The Yugoslavian political and economic system of "market socialism" is merely a case in point. And such American phenomena as country clubs establish that some collective goods (a jointly owned golf course, for example) can be privately owned and supported through a market for membership.

---

[4]See also William J. Baumol, *Welfare Economics and the Theory of the State,* Cambridge: Harvard University Press, 1952.

More important is the avoidance of a second erroneous conclusion: that all collective goods are "natural" occurrences, and thus objects that concretely define an inevitable limit to any market system. Perhaps some collective goods, such as "a state of domestic tranquility" or the "ending of an epidemic" may appear naturally nonexcludable in our society, but technology and economic arrangements are always intervening variables. Consider the existence of a terrible epidemic. The affected population receives the threat collectively. But there may be various means of *private* exit from the threatening situation: migration, innoculation, etc., all of which may be as effective as the ending of the epidemic in avoiding the disease. Many of these private good alternatives could be marketed and thus serve as substitutes (for at least some of the people) for the problem of finding a collective solution.

Indeed, the first thing the terminology forces us to note is the existence of a relationship between the market structure of a society and its use of collective action in the solving of its problems. Thus, if markets allow for the individual purchase of private solutions to collective problems, there may never be a collectively supplied solution to the problem. Political action may become quite unnecessary, and yet some individuals may never be in the position of purchasing the private solution. Analogously, we can supply on a non-excludable basis what are normally considered private goods. That is, we can collectively supply goods that are divisible. In other words, although we have lumped excludability and divisibility together as defining characteristics of collective goods, these variables are really independent of each other.[5] We can conceive of divisible goods supplied collectively (health insurance, housing, food, etc.) and indivisible goods supplied in a market and hence with an exclusion mechanism (a club's golf course, a theater performance, etc.). In the latter case, access to a shared item is what is bought or sold in the market.

Of course, some goods may be more difficult to supply through a market than others. But even defense against nuclear attack (which may be thought of as a virtually *pure* collective good) has its market potential. Recall the sale of private bomb shelters to the wealthy American public during the 1950's. Still, there is some appeal to the notion that given any particular technological achievements and social arrangements, there will be some goods that are more purely collective than others. Thus, the distinction between private and collective goods is itself relativized by the technological and social arrangements of a society.

By examining the definitional characteristics of collective goods, and by employing the psychological assumption of rational behavior, we will show what forces an individual to make sacrifices for the obtaining of a

[5]The distinction between divisibility and excludability was not properly made in the original articles by Samuelson (cited in fn 3). Later articles and works developed variables at issue. See J. G. Head, "Public Goods and Public Policy," *Public Finance*, XVII, No. 3, 1962, pp. 197–219 and Mancur Olson, *op. cit.*, pp. 14, 36–43 where he discusses excludability and distinguishes between exclusive and inclusive groups. The usage in this context stems from earlier work of the authors, especially, "A Reformulation of the Collective Good-Private Good Distinction," paper given at the 1972 *Public Choice Society Annual Meetings*, Pittsburgh.

collective good. From this stems a number of laws of political organizing regarding what must be done if a group is to receive collective goods, or have their common interests satisfied.

II. INDIVIDUAL BEHAVIOR AND OPTIMALITY

Let us examine the problems people face in obtaining collective goods. First, under what conditions will individuals obtain the optimal amount of a collective good? To answer this question we need a definition of "optimal amount." If we could identify the "optimal" or most preferred alternative for a rational individual, then by definition (of rational) we would determine what alternative he would choose. But we must note that what is optimal, or best, for the individual may not be best for the group.

And we are interested in the outcome for groups of individuals: the consequences of group choices. Is it guaranteed that when all members of a group choose the *individually optimal alternative,* the result is optimal for the group of individuals? That is, will rational individuals "naturally" behave in a manner consistent with their group interests? The answer to this question clearly is of critical importance to the analysis of political behavior. To answer it, and subsequent derivative questions, we will examine in greater detail what is meant by an individual optimum, or the alternative to be chosen by rational individuals. To do this, we shall employ graphical techniques.

Begin with a simple, yet general, decision problem: how much of any good is it rational to buy? Rationality allows us to specify that the level which gives the individual the greatest net benefits will be most preferred by the individuals. In other words, the individual wants to maximize his net gains or net benefits. If he *prefers* to increase his net gains and is rational, he will *choose* that level that does maximize his net gains. To see the implications of this, consider more carefully what is involved in *maximizing net gains.*

Net gains are the difference between total benefits that accrue to an individual from the choice of any alternative and the total costs involved in choosing that alternative. Call total benefits, *TB;* total costs, *TC;* and net benefits *NB.* Algebraically:

$$NB = TB - TC$$

and the individual who is rational will seek to maximize this expression.

To illustrate, imagine that in a particular community, the real estate tax level is $1 for every $100 of assessed value of the real estate. For example, an individual with a home assessed at $20,000 must pay $200 a year tax. Imagine a tax assessor who must appraise the properties of a landlord owning millions of dollars of land in this town. It might be possible for the landlord to bribe the assessor to keep the assessed value of his properties low. Indeed, if the assessor is not caught, the two of them can benefit considerably by making a deal. The assessor, of course, is taking quite a risk. And the larger the decreased assessment on the properties, the greater the risk. For the assessor's supervisor may not notice an assessment that is only a few thousand dollars too low, but he is likely to notice one that is many thousand dollars low. For the landlord, the value of each hundred dollars decrease in assessment is identical: $1. But, if the assessor requires increasing payments to compensate for increased risks, then each hundred dollars decrease will be more expensive than the previous one. This is sufficient information for us to be able to develop a graphical representation of the total cost for the wealthy landlord.[6] In Figure 2–1, the vertical axis represents (the landlord's) costs and benefits, while the horizontal axis represents the quantity purchased or size of the deal made with the assessor, i.e. the decrease in the assessed value of the landlord's properties. In the graph, the total cost curve is upward sloping and ever steeper for higher levels of purchases. Can we see why? What does the slope of this line represent? It represents how the total cost changes with respect to the change in the level of assessment. For example, if we pick two different levels of "deals" (h and j, where j is a bigger deal than h) we can see how the total cost curve must change at h and j. For the assessor requires that each $100 deal be more expensive than the previous one. So at h, the cost

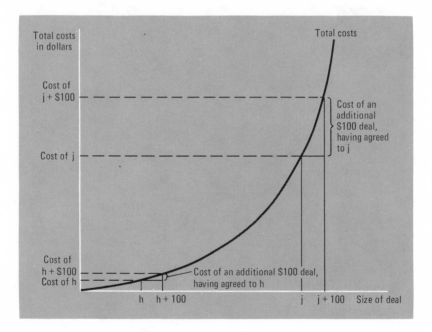

Figure 2–1   Total cost to landlord

[6]Note that the particular shapes of the total-cost and total-benefit functions are not appropriate for all situations. For a consumer in a market, the total-benefit curve normally is assumed to be curved and the total cost curve is linear. The basic analysis would not change for other "reasonable" shapes. See Frohlich et al, "Individual Contributions to Collective Goods: Alternative Models," *Journal of Conflict Resolution,* XIX, No. 2, June 1975, pp. 310–30.

of moving to a deal of size "$h + \$100$" is less than the cost of moving from j to "$j + \$100$". Thus, in Figure 2–1, a $100 change on the horizontal axis at h causes the total-cost curve to rise less than at j. Or the slope of the total-cost curve keeps getting steeper as we move to the right.

We will see that "how the total-cost curve changes at any point" is a crucial concept in the development of rational choice. Economists have given it a special name: *marginal cost.* [7] Marginal cost, or the slope of the cost line, represents the cost of the next purchase by the landlord. But to decide on the optimal level of purchase, he must consider not only costs but also benefits. We assumed that for every $100 decrease in assessed value agreed to by the assessor, the total benefits to the landlord increase by $1. In such a case, the total benefit line would be an upward sloping, straight line (see Figure 2–2). As the size of the deal made with the assessor goes up, so does the total benefit. The benefit per dollar of deal made with the assessor is constant. So the *TB* line in the graph rises $1 for every $100 deal and is linear and increasing. Here again the economists employ the notion of

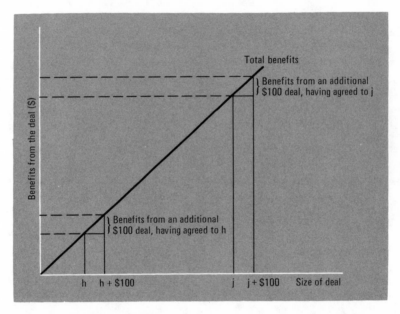

Figure 2–2   Total benefits to landlord

[7]For those with mathematical skills beyond elementary algebra, the discussion of marginal cost (and marginal benefit below) is likely to have been belabored. The concept of marginal cost can be translated into the language of calculus: marginal cost is the first derivative of the total-cost function, with respect to quantity supplied: $d(TC)/dQ$. Marginal benefit is likewise the derivative of the benefit function. Furthermore, some of the other relationships derived below are direct consequences when one employs calculus. A fine introductory treatment to these concepts for those who know calculus can be found in J. M. Henderson and R. E. Quandt, *Microeconomics Theory,* New York: McGraw-Hill, 1958.

"margin" and refer to the benefits gained from an incremental deal as the *marginal benefits.* Once again the concept refers to "how the total benefit curve changes at any point." More generally:

> *Marginal cost* is the cost of a one unit change in the level of purchase and *marginal benefit* is the benefit associated with a one unit change in the level of purchase.

We must now discover how the landlord's interest in increasing his net benefit relates to these two concepts of marginal cost and marginal benefit.

Recall that net benefits, for any particular level of purchase of the good, is the difference between total benefit and total cost. Graphically the net benefit is the vertical distance between the total benefit and the total cost lines (see Figure 2–3). If the total benefit line is above the total cost line, then the point of maximum vertical distance between the two lines is the individual's optimum level of purchase. This level is marked with "opt." in Figure 2–3.

At this level of purchase, the benefit and cost lines are parallel to one another: their slopes are the same. But recall that these slopes represent the marginal cost and marginal benefit associated with all possible deals for the landlord. Thus, the optimum occurs where:

1. the vertical distance between benefits and costs is greatest (providing bene· fits are higher than costs).

But this means that:

2. the slopes of the cost and benefit lines are the same: they are parallel.

Finally this implies that:

3. marginal cost = marginal benefit.[8]

Thus, the *maximum-benefit point occurs where the marginal benefit equals the marginal cost. The rational individual will reach an equilibrium by purchasing to that level. Choosing that level is choosing the best alternative—the optimal choice.*

If individuals are assumed to behave rationally, they are assumed to behave in this fashion. To see how such individually rational behavior relates to group behavior we combine the behaviors of individually rational persons interacting to obtain a common interest or collective good. Consider another example: assume that a producer seeks (from the government) an increase in the price support for his product. The price support, we assume, is in the form of a guaranteed minimum price for the products which he supplies. Such programs are common in a variety of political arenas and are often the result of group action. In the United States, for example, such supports exist for a variety of agricultural products. They

---

[8]Note that this is equivalent to requiring that the two derivatives are equal: $d(TC)/dQ = d(TB)/dQ$ for the maximum.

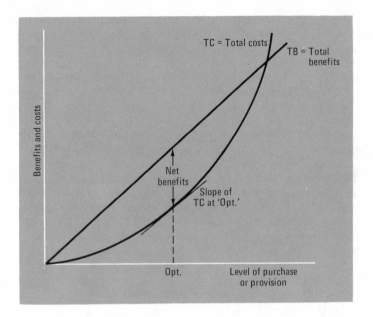

At 'Opt.', or the optimal level of purchase, the slope of the total cost line (TC) = the slope of the total benefit line (TB). 'Opt.' is also where the vertical distance (or net benefits) between the lines is maximized.

Figure 2–3   Individual optimality

allow the farmer to receive a guaranteed price for all of his crop. If the consumers in the market will not purchase the product at a sufficiently high price, the government purchases the remainder at the agreed upon price support level. Since price supports are valuable to producers, promises of such supports are sometimes used by politicians to gain support and revenues for political campaigns.

Indeed, in a recent well publicized case involving increased price supports for milk, milk producers seem to have been involved in a *quid pro quo* exchange with the Nixon Administration. They apparently contributed $300,000 to Nixon's 1972 presidential election campaign, and, in return received a 26 cents per hundredweight increase in price supports.[9] Conceivably, the producers could have increased or decreased their contributions to gain greater or smaller changes in the price supports. Was the amount purchased the optimal amount? If not, what would be·the optimal change in support levels for the producers? How does one go about calculating the optimal level of supply of any good?

To develop the answers to these questions, imagine that the dairy industry is dominated by a single monopolistic producer. Assume that the

[9]William Shannon, *The New York Times*, Sept. 1972. As he put it, "that meant $500 million to $700 million more for dairy farmers in the new marketing year."

producer is interested in supplying himself with the best possible (i.e., optimal) level of price supports and that these are to be obtained from the president in exchange for donations to the presidential campaign. (Later, other producers can be introduced into the example to see how a group differs from an individual.) The milk producer's decision as to how much to contribute will be predicated on the relative costs and benefits of the possible levels of contributions. From the previous paragraphs, we know he will choose to maximize his total net benefits. To do this he will have to evaluate the net effect of each *additional* purchase of an increased level of price supports. For each level, he will have to compare the marginal benefit with the marginal cost. If the marginal benefit is larger than the marginal cost, he would gain from the additional purchase and so we can assume he makes that purchase. Thus, he stops purchasing just before marginal cost exceeds marginal benefit. This insures him that each penny increase is profitable. To analyze his calculations, let us fill in the situation with hypothetical details. Let Table 2–1 represent the various costs and benefits of different levels of contribution and associated "purchasable" changes in price supports.

Here we assume that the dairyman produces a fixed output of 500,000 hundredweight of milk. If the monopolist expects the market price of milk to be below the current level of price supports, each cent increase in the price-support yields a $5,000 rise in his income. (Column E represents the rise in income for a *change* of 1 cent at each level of price supports. This *rise in income for each penny rise in price support level* is the marginal benefit.)

Of course, any rise in the price-support is purchased at the cost of a contribution to the campaign. In calculating the optimal price-support purchase, the monopolist must take these costs into account. Assume the costs reflect the likelihood that the President would have to be paid increasingly

Table 2–1   A Rational Monopolist Buying Changes in Price Supports

(A) Increased Price Support per Hundredweight	(B) Total Gross Benefit	−	(C) Total Cost	=	(D) Total Net Benefit	(E) Marginal Benefit	−	(F) Marginal Cost	=	(G) Marginal Net Benefit
$0.00	$ 0,000		$ 000							
						$5,000		$1,500		$3,500
0.01	5,000		1,500		$3,500					
						5,000		3,000		2,000
0.02	10,000		4,500		5,500					
						5,000*		4,500*		500*
0.03	15,000		9,000*		6,000*					
						5,000		6,000		−1,000
0.04	20,000		15,000		5,000					
						5,000		7,500		−2,500
0.05	25,000		22,500		2,500					
						5,000		9,000		−4,000
0.06	30,000		31,500		1,500					

*represents the optimal level

higher sums to adopt increasingly unpopular positions. Notice each additional 1 cent support costs more than did the previous one. In other words, the marginal cost is rising; see Column *F*. But the dairyman considers the difference between marginal cost and marginal benefit as is captured in the marginal net benefit (cf. Column *G*). By focusing on marginal net benefit, we can say that *it is rational to purchase* additional price supports *as long as the marginal net benefit is positive.* By doing this, he accumulates a total net benefit that corresponds to the *sum of all of his* marginal net benefits.[10] The calculus outlined enables him to *maximize his total net benefit.* In this example he will purchase 3 cents of price supports. This results in a total net benefit of $6,000, the maximum possible in Column *D*. If the monopolist purchased the fourth cent of price support, it would yield a marginal net benefit of—$1000, i.e., a net loss. This is reflected in a total net benefit of $5,000: $1,000 less than if he had stopped his purchases at 3 cents.

Rational individuals are assumed to behave in this fashion.[11] Now let us use these findings to identify implications of rational behavior for aggregate action and the provision of collective goods to groups of individuals.

III. COLLECTIVE BEHAVIOR AND SUBOPTIMALITY[12]

Suppose each individual in a group is a potential recipient of a collective good. Each acts so as to maximize his own net benefit. Will the sum of these actions result in a rational or optimal set of actions for the group as a whole? In other words, will individual rationality lead the group to consequences that maximize the benefits of the members of the group? No matter how it is phrased, the question is the same and the answer is no. Except under special conditions, whenever there are a number of individuals, all of whom are acting with regard to a shared objective, the results are not optimal.

[10]The student of calculus will see that this follows directly from the fact that the marginal benefits are the first derivative of total benefits. Hence the integral of the marginal benefits will be total benefits.

[11]Of course, we once again are reminded that there is no necessary link between rationality and morality. To many, the activities of the special interest lobbies are the height of immorality. That needn't disqualify them from being rational. See the Introduction to Part I for a fuller discussion of this issue.

[12]In the discussion that follows, a number of simplifications have been made for the purposes of exposition. Traditionally, what are called "income effects" of one individual's purchase of the collective good on the other individual's decisions have been included in all derivations. Furthermore, the arguments here are developed using the notion of a monetary resource in terms of which we can evaluate each individual's benefits. These assumptions greatly facilitate the exposition, making unnecessary the use of indifference curves, etc. On the other hand, the assumptions are unnecessarily (from a theoretical point of view) restrictive. Students interested in further theoretical work on these problems should examine some of the more "standard" expositions. In particular, those mentioned in fn 3 (supra). Also see, Mancur Olson and Richar Zeckhauser, "An Economic Theory of Alliances," *The Review of Economics and Statistics*, **48**:3, August 1966, pp. 266–79; John Chamberlain, "Provision of Collective Goods as a Function of Group Size," *American Political Science Review*, **68**:2, June 1974, pp. 707–16; and Martin C. McGuire, "Group Size, Group Homogeneity and the Aggregate Provision of a Pure Public Good under Cournot Behavior," *Public Choice*, XVIII, Spring 1974, pp. 107–26.

To illustrate this line of argument, let us introduce into our milk producer example a small milk producer, producing one fourth as much as the original producer.

Assume the situation to be identical to that pictured earlier in the following respects: (1) the big dairy does not change its production of milk, (2) the costs of price supports are unchanged, (3) the benefits to the big dairy of the price supports are the same. But the situation is different in one respect: The additional dairy will also get benefits from any change in price supports. Thus, the small dairy's benefits increase the *total* benefits accruing from any price supports.

What can we say about rational behavior of each of the producers now? What is the relationship of the aggregate actions of the producers to rational group behavior?

Table 2-2 represents the costs and benefits to the small dairy of any purchase of a change of price-support levels. The benefits consist of its output (one fourth of the 500,000 hundredweights produced by the big dairy, or 125,000 hundredweights of milk) times the price increase per hundredweight. That is, the small diary will gain $1250 per 1 cent increase in price supports (cf. column D, Table 2-2). Its marginal benefit is $1,250. But the cost of any 1 cent increase (cf. Column E) is the same for the small and the big dairy. And these marginal costs are always greater than $1,250. That is, marginal benefit is always less than marginal cost. Clearly, the small dairy will not find it worthwhile to pay for any price supports. Unless the two dairymen are organized to *share* the costs of the price supports, the small producer will pay nothing toward the changed level of supports. Only the big dairy will purchase supports, even though the benefits of any changes will be collectively supplied to the other member of the industry. The big dairy, faced with an unchanged income situation (cf. Table 2-1), will

Table 2-2   A Rational "Small" Producer Buying Price Supports

(A) Increased Price Supports per Hundredweight	(B) Total Gross Benefit	(C) Total Cost	(D) Marginal Benefit	(E) Marginal Cost
$0.00*	$0,000	$ 000		
			$1,250	$1,500
0.01	1,250	1,500		
			1,250	3,000
0.02	2,500	4,500		
			1,250	4,500
0.03	3,750	9,000*		
			1,250	6,000
0.04	5,000	15,000		
			1,250	7,500
0.05	6,250	22,500		
			1,250	9,000
0.06	7,500	31,500		

*represents the optimal level to be purchased by the small producer.

continue to buy a 3-cent increase in the supports. Such a purchase yields a $3,750 benefit to the small dairy.

But is a 3-cent level of price supports the optimal level for the group as a whole? To answer this question, we must ascertain what benefits and costs accrue to the group as a whole from each level of price support.

In general, the benefits received by the group are the sum of the benefits received by each of the members (see Table 2–3). Thus Column D, the marginal benefit to the group, is the sum of the marginal benefits in the previous two tables. One can see that for the group as a whole the marginal benefits exceed the marginal cost (Column E) for purchases of up to 4 cents of price supports. At that level the group gets a *total net benefit*, the difference between Columns B and C, of $10,000, which is the maximum possible. This figure declines for higher levels of price supports.

We know that the small firm acting on its own will not purchase any price supports. Moreover, in buying increased price supports, the large dairy will continue to buy increased levels of price supports only until *its* marginal cost approaches *its* marginal benefits. Each single purchaser will *not* take into account the benefits accruing to the other members of the industry. Thus, without any arrangements to share the costs of additional purchases, the net result of the individual rational behavior in this situation will be suboptimal for the group. And the *suboptimality means* that *both* producers *could conceivably have been made better off* by the purchase of a fourth penny's increase in price supports. That is, they could have had some distribution of the cost of the additional purchase so that they both would have been able to gain. For example, if the small dairy were to pay $1,100 and the large dairy were to pay $4,900, together the $6,000 could cover the marginal cost involved with the fourth cent of price support. And that additional cent support would yield a marginal benefit of $1250 for the small

Table 2–3   A Rational Level for Buying Price Supports of Both Producers as a Group

(A) Price Supports per Hundredweight	(B) Total Gross Benefits	(C) Total Cost	(D) Marginal Benefit	(E) Marginal Cost
$0.00	$ 0,000	$ 000		
			$6,250	$1,500
0.01	6,250	1,500		
			6,250	3,000
0.02	12,500	4,500		
			6,250	4,500
0.03	18,750	9,000		
			6,250	6,000
0.04*	25,000	15,000		
			6,250	7,500
0.05	31,250	22,500		
			6,250	9,000
0.06	37,500	31,500		

*represents the optimal level

dairy and $5,000 for the large dairy. *They would both profit.* But without a means for cost sharing, rational behavior on their parts will lead to the nonattainment of these benefits!

Let us generalize these results using graphical techniques. To analyze a situation involving more than one individual, sharing the same collective good, there must be one (common) cost curve, and a separate benefit curve for each individual.

For simplicity, Figure 2–4 represents a situation involving only two individuals with different valuations of the good. Individual 1 is like the big dairy whose benefits exceed costs over some range. Individual 2 is like the small dairy for whom costs always exceed benefits. For both of them total costs (the curved line) are positive and increasing, and marginal costs (the slope of the cost line) is increasing. Marginal benefits are assumed to be positive and constant so that the individual total benefit lines are straight: the slope is a constant. We can identify the individual optima in this example

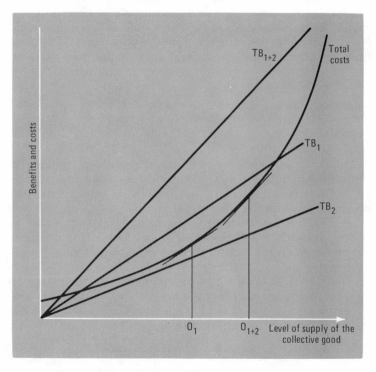

TB_1 = individual 1's total benefits for all levels of supply of X

TB_2 = individual 2's total benefits for all levels of supply of X

TB_{1+2} = the group's total benefits for all levels of supply of X as we did in Figure 2-3. For individual 1 it occurs at O_1 [where the slope of total costs (the marginal cost) is equal to the slope of TB, (the marginal benefit)]. For individual 2 the optimum occurs at "no purchase" because for him cost always exceeds benefit. The determination of the group optimum requires a group valuation curve. This curve is the vertical sum of TB_1 and TB_2, called TB_{1+2}. From it, the group optimum O_{1+2} can be calculated.

In Figure 2-4, the group optimum can be seen to occur at a higher level of supply than either of the individual optima. This is because the benefit to the group is *the sum* of the individual benefits. As such, it is higher than any one individual's benefits. Thus, neither individual *acting alone* will bring the group to an optimal level of supply. Rather the rational individual chooses *his* most preferred alternative to maximize *his* welfare. The unorganized actions of a group of such individuals will not maximize the welfare of the group as a whole. For the *total benefits* of the collective good *are shared* by the members of the group, but the *costs are not.* Individual decisions by rational individuals lead to suboptimal results.

The results are now obviously generalizable.[13] They do not depend upon the particular placements of the optima of the individuals concerned. Nor does the suboptimality depend upon the consideration of merely two individuals as in the example. In general, we can note the following law of politics:

If a group of individuals who share, or could share, the benefits of a collective good are not organized to share the costs of obtaining the good, they will receive suboptimal amounts of the good.

We can derive an important corollary by slightly expanding the analysis yielding this law. Suppose we consider situations like those above except with different numbers of small dairies. What would happen if the industry contained not one small dairy but say 10, or 100 or 1000? Each individual dairy would have the same marginal benefit of $1,250 per 1-cent increase in supports, and each would find it irrational to buy any price supports. Thus, the amount of price support that the group would supply itself (without any provision for cost sharing) would not vary as the number of small producers increased. But as the group contained more dairies, the marginal *group* benefits from each level of price supports would increase and so the optimal level of price supports would rise. Thus the constant level of supply would imply that as the group became larger, the amount by which the

---

[13]The careful reader may have noticed that there is another assumption lurking in the background to this argument. We are assuming that each individual is motivated by the payoffs he or she receives directly, and is not motivated by altruism. For example, we assumed that each dairy owner only asked about his own profits, rather than the profits of his competitors. Similarly, we assume that there are no other forms of interaction between the benefits received by one individual and the vicarious pleasure received by another. This assumption can be relaxed, but under certain forms of altruism (in particular the unanimous adoption of the Christian ethic ("do onto others as you would have them do onto you"), the general law no longer holds. For a thorough discussion of this see Norman Frohlich, "Self-Interest or Altruism, What Difference?" *Journal of Conflict Resolution,* **18**, No. 1, March 1974, pp. 55–73.

group fell short of optimal supply would increase. This conclusion can be stated generally as a corollary to the law stated above:

The larger the number of individuals in an unorganized group, the more suboptimal will be their receipt of collective goods.

Perhaps the overwhelming political centrality of these conclusions should be underscored. The results extend beyond the crass bribery of governmental officials to obtain special loopholes and programs. Remember that the satisfaction of *any common interest* is a collective good. The first law of politics asserts that unless the group is organized all common interests will be suboptimally satisfied. The second law says that the larger the unorganized group, the greater the deprivation.

Assuming the citizen is the best judge of his own welfare, we can identify a constitutional rule necessary for the general welfare of the citizens. Those civil liberties and social conditions insuring individuals the right to organize themselves to share in the costs of pursuing collective interests are necessary for the continued welfare of the citizenry. To deprive a group of people merely requires taking away its ability to organize politically. Deny workers the right to organize unions, deny prisoners the opportunity to organize a political protest of their conditions, deny the poor the resources to communicate with each other, and you effectively deny them the ability to remedy their political problems. The larger the deprived group, the greater the deprivation.

So it is not surprising that Mancur Olson concluded his original derivation of these arguments as follows:

> The remaining type of group is the unorganized group—the group that has no lobby and takes no action. Groups of this kind fit the main argument of this book best of all. They illustrate its central point: that large or latent groups have no tendency voluntarily to act to further their common interests. This point was asserted in the Introduction and it is with this point that the study must conclude. For the unorganized groups, the groups that have no lobbies and exert no pressure, are among the largest groups in the nation, and they have some of the most vital common interests.
>
> Migrant farm laborers are a significant group with urgent common interests, and they have no lobby to voice their needs. The white-collar workers are a large group with common interests, but they have no organization to care for their interests. . . . There are multitudes with an interest in peace, but they have no lobby to match those of the "special interests" that may on occasion have an interest in war. . . .
>
> Nor can such groups be expected to organize or act simply because the gains from group action would exceed the costs . . . . [The] rational individual in the large [unorganized] group in a socio-political context will not be willing to make any sacrifices to achieve the objectives he shares with others.[14]

[14]Olson, *op. cit.*, pp. 165–66.

IV. FOR FURTHER READING

Most obvious from the footnotes is the centrality of Mancur Olson, Jr., *The Logic of Collective Action*. Beyond containing theoretical arguments it includes interesting applications of the theory to the writings of Marx and various important sectors of American life, including migrant labor, labor unions, the AMA, etc. Extensions of Olson's analysis, are given in footnotes 3 and 12.

Perhaps the best known application of the theory is Olson and Zeckhauser's "An Economic Theory of Alliances," (cf. footnote 12). James M. Buchanan's "An Economic Theory of Clubs," *Economica*, Feb. 1965, Vol. 32, pp. 1–14, also deserves attention. A recent, and unusually imaginative application of the theory is contained in N. I. Fainstein and S. S. Fainstein, *Urban Political Movements*, Englewood Cliffs: Prentice-Hall, 1974.

CHAPTER THREE

COLLECTIVE ACTION, MARGINAL COST SHARING, AND CONTINGENT PREFERENCES

Unorganized groups fail to supply themselves with optimal amounts of collective goods. Optimality requires cost sharing, and politically unorganized individuals have no explicit means of coordinating their actions to share the costs of providing a collective good. Each person chooses a course of action with neither constraints nor incentives placed upon him by the group. Each individual stops purchasing additional amounts of the good when *he* no longer values the next "bit" more than the cost of supplying it, regardless of the benefits the group might receive from that purchase. The result is suboptimal supply.

Some form of organization of the recipients to share the costs of the goods is needed to achieve optimal supply. The trick is to organize the group to distribute the costs of the goods among the people who receive the benefits. Cost sharing is necessary if optimal supply is to be achieved. But is it enough? In other words, in the absence of extrinsic punishments or rewards associated with behavior by individuals, is a cost-sharing arrangement a guarantee of optimality? Or is something else needed, some other conditions, without which cost sharing will fail to solve group suboptimalities? There may be a variety of contexts and types of cost sharing, only some of which may prove to be effective. To be effective, any arrangement must make it worthwhile for individuals to contribute when, in the absence of the scheme, they would fail to do so, or else it would simply be unable to move the group toward optimality.

To begin, let us examine the possibility that some cost-sharing agreements fail to give individuals the necessary incentive to contribute. In our example, no individual values the collective good enough to purchase any of it on his own.[1] Thus, *some* form of cost sharing is imperative if *any* of the good is to be provided. It will soon be apparent that not just any form of cost sharing will do the trick.

Ten migrant farmworkers are under a week's contract to harvest a farmer's perishable grape crop. The crop is exceptionally good and labor is in short supply. The farmer is lucky to get the 10 persons and especially fortunate to get them for a full week. The workers will have to work full time to get his crop picked without spoilage. But they are dissatisfied with their wages (calculated on a piecework basis). On the average, each picks enough grapes per hour to receive an effective hourly wage of $1.50. Even though they did not know each other before the contract was signed, the workers all get together for a few beers after the first day's work. As they talk, it is apparent that all of them are dissatisfied. They conclude that they should receive a bonus, not calculated on piecework, for the week's work. Anticipating that the farmer will disagree, they plan to bring pressure to bear to get the farmer to meet their demands. Their strategy calls for them to share the cost of putting on the pressure. They will demand an extra $5 per person. If refused, the workers agree to engage in a one-hour work "slowdown." This slowdown would result in the spoilage of some of the farmer's crop. After the slowdown they would again place their demand before the farmer. But, these plans are not self-executing. Indeed, to the extent that they pick fewer grapes, they receive less income. Success in this action depends on the voluntary cooperation of the group of workers. They do not plan to impose any threats (or rewards) on each other. Indeed, we can assume working conditions that make them unable to "check up" on each other. Therefore, they expect each worker to participate because of his valuation of the collectively bargained for bonus.

In the morning, they demand the $5 bonus and threaten to pick only one third the usual quantity of grapes between 11 a.m. and noon if refused. Such a slowdown would result in the spoilage of two thirds of an hour's harvest (say $500 worth of grapes). It also causes each worker to lose ⅔ of the $1.50 he can earn by picking at normal rates. The farmer is quick to appreciate his potential loss, but he also notes the wage loss each worker suffers in a slowdown. After a moment's deliberation the farmer refuses to pay the bonus. The farmer's foreman is aghast. "How," he asks, "is it worth your while to risk a $500 loss to save the $50 demanded by the workers?"

"I won't lose a penny. When those workers think about it each one will realize that it's not worth his while to participate," responds the farmer. This does not convince the foreman, however, and they watch and wonder what will happen between 11 and noon in each worker's section of the vineyard.

Consider how the workers will act, given their previous discussion and agreement. In particular, under what conditions would the farmer be right

---

[1]This situation is similar to the position of the dairies after 3 cents of price supports have been purchased. It is in no one's interest to purchase price supports on his own, yet the supply is suboptimal. The distinction between groups in which an individual values the good enough to supply some of it on his own and groups in which no member has such high valuations was first made by Mancur Olson, *The Logic of Collective Action*, Cambridge: Harvard University Press, 1965, pp. 48–50. He suggestively called groups with individuals who place such high value on the collective goods "privileged groups."

in his assessment that the workers' joint action will fail? Under what conditions would he be wrong? Which sorts of cost-sharing arrangements will lead to a successful slowdown and which will fail?

Consider the thoughts and projections of any one of the workers. There are two ways in which the slowdown can be perceived as affecting the farmer. Each worker might believe that he can contribute to the overall leverage brought to bear on the farmer: the more workers who slowdown, the larger are the concessions they can wring from the farmer. On the other hand, the worker could imagine that a specific threshold of pressure is required to obtain the desired bonus. If the threshold isn't reached, the farmer won't give in: all or nothing.[2] These two possibilities reflect different conceptions of how the individual contributions relate to the collective effort. They reflect different conceptions of cost sharing. And these alternate conceptions have potentially very different consequences.

Suppose each worker expects that the objective will be obtained at a variable level in proportion to the level of contributions received. To illustrate, imagine that a worker projects (1) if all workers slowdown, they each get a $5 bonus and (2) the size of the realizable (and realized) bonus in other situations is proportional to the number of individuals who participate in the slowdown. Thus, if 3 workers (or 30 percent) slowdown, they can expect to gain only 30 percent of $5 per person (i.e., $1.50). The numbers are merely illustrative. How does such a view effect the strategic choice of the worker?

Using these simplified figures, we can identify the type of calculation underlying the decision of each worker to support or not to support the slowdown. To participate in the slowdown, each worker must give up $1 in wages. This is his share of the marginal cost of getting the $5 bonus. The payoffs to each worker, associated with each of their possible strategy choices, can be calculated and represented as in Table 3–1.

Each strategic alternative is represented by a row. Any worker's return from his choice of action depends upon the actions of all of the other workers. That is, the return is contingent on the action of the others. These contingencies are represented as columns in the table. For example, if the worker in question supports the slowdown while nine others do likewise, he will get a *net* return of $4.00 (the $5.00 bonus obtained by the successful

Table 3–1   Net Payoffs Going to the Worker if *x* Others Support the Slowdown*

		Number of others who support the slowdown (X) =					
		9	8	...	2	1	0
INDIVIDUAL STRATEGIC OPTIONS	Support	$4.00	$3.50	...	$0.50	$0.00	-$0.50
	Defect	$4.50	$4.00	...	$1.00	$0.50	$0.00

*All entries are calculated as follows: (1) for the support strategy: [maximum bonus ($5) *x* proportion of workers supporting slowdown (*X* + 1)] – cost of participation in lost wages ($1), or: $0.50 (*X* + 1) – $1. and (2) for the defect strategy: maximum bonus ($5) *x* proportion of workers supporting the slowdown when he doesn't, or: $0.50*X*.

[2] In this case, each donation could be thought of as increasing the odds of reaching, or going over the threshhold. This will be developed further in Sections II and III of this chapter.

action minus the $1.00 lost in piecework caused by participation in the slowdown). If only eight others slowdown, the net return is cut by 50 cents to $3.50. This payoff is shown in the second column of the table. Each of the different numbers of others who might participate in the slowdown represent a different contingency and hence are represented by a different column.

Examine Table 3–1. In *each column* the payoff to the worker is bigger if he doesn't support the slowdown. Each worker finds it advantageous to defect and not participate *in all contingencies. No matter what he expects the others to do, he is better off if he does not participate in the slowdown.* Why? Because although each worker's participation contributes an additional $5 bonus to be shared by members of the group, it only yields 50 cents for the individual. And participation in the slowdown costs the worker $1 in lost wages. Thus, *participation is a losing proposition for each individual.* Every worker defects and fails to support the slowdown. Collective action fizzles and nothing comes from the plans. And yet, this is clearly not optimal for the group.[3] Each worker's $1 cost could have brought $5 of total benefits to the group. Group benefits outweigh costs.

But failure is predictable because each worker perceives his effort as being a distinctive incremental contribution to the good. Thus, he compares the marginal gain *he* gets from the effort with the overall marginal cost of supplying that increment. *And that cost is entirely his* marginal cost. He does not share the cost of the increment with others. This is precisely the characteristic used to derive the conclusion regarding suboptimal supply in the previous chapter.

Thus this attempt to share the costs does not change the individual's incentive to contribute to the collective good. Rational individuals would *not* voluntarily contribute even if such a scheme were agreed to in advance. No individual finds the benefits that follow from *his* marginal contribution greater than the marginal cost *he* is asked to bear to achieve that benefit. Therefore, this cost-sharing scheme is insufficient to secure the group's collective interests.

What went wrong? Each worker shares the benefits but foots the entire cost of each marginal increment. But this very failing gives us a clue to how the cost-sharing arrangement could be changed to be potentially successful. If it were arranged that individuals *shared* the *marginal* cost (i.e. the cost of *each* increment), the incentive to contribute could be increased. The benefit

---

[3]Situations similar to the one depicted are often called *prisoner-dilemma games.* The first person to show the precise relationship between "the logic of collective action" and prisoner dilemma games was Russell Hardin, "Collective Action as an Agreeable *n*-Prisoners' Dilemma," *Behavioral Science,* **16,** Sept.–Oct. 1971, pp. 472–481. The relationship was pointed out earlier by Robert Axelrod, *Conflict of Interest,* Chicago: Markham 1970, Chap. 3.

The analysis of such games is a fascinating subject in itself. For a good introductory account the reader might examine Thomas Schelling, "Hockey Helmets, Concealed Weapons, and Daylight Saving: A Study of Binary Choice with Externalities," *Journal of Conflict Resolution,* **17,** Sept. 1973, pp. 381–428. But not all collective action situations need be prisoner dilemmas. Frohlich et al. "Individual Contributions to Collective Goods: Alternative Models," *Journal of Conflict Resolution,* June 1975 and Russell Hardin "Group Provision of Step Goods," *Behavioral Science,* **21,** 1976, pp. 101–106.

of a contribution is, after all, fixed. If the cost *of each increment* were shared, an individual's marginal benefit could outweigh his marginal cost. That is, individuals could find it worthwhile to contribute.

If rational individuals are voluntarily to contribute for collective goods, they must share marginal cost. Successful political organization, therefore, requires *sharing the marginal cost of each additional unit of the collective good.* The cost of each "lumpy bit" of the good provided must be shared among the individuals. Marginal cost sharing won't guarantee success, but it is *necessary* for successful organizing.

I. ORGANIZING FOR MARGINAL COST SHARING: ESTABLISHING A THRESHOLD

How can marginal cost sharing be instituted among the workers? The most direct method would be to agree to pool the day's earnings and divide the group's wages equally among the members. This would mean that any individual who reduces his pick to support the slowdown will be subsidized by those who do not. Such a pooling of wages, we should remark, would not be self-enforcing and hence requires some incentive other than the collective good itself.[4] Suppose the workers do not agree to pool their earnings? Are they doomed to failure? Not necessarily.

Earlier each and every contribution to the slowdown increased the size of the bonus that the group could receive. This notion was based on a subjective estimation of the behavior of the farmer. But it was formally incorporated in the worker's calculations of the returns expected from his alternative strategies. The workers could have other expectations. More explicitly, they could believe the conclusion that if *enough* of them engage in the slowdown, the farmer will yield to their $5 demand; but if they do not show that degree of solidarity of purpose, their cause is lost and the farmer will concede nothing. Such a situation can be engineered by reaching a conditional agreement the night before. For example, one worker could volunteer to be the spokesperson for the group if, and only if, enough others end up supporting him by engaging in the slowdown.[5] In other words, the final demand would be put to the farmer only if enough workers agree to and actually participate in the slowdown. If he is believed, he will have changed the workers' perceptions of what it will take to supply the collective good. For under that arrangement, unless a certain threshold of collective action is reached, no concessions will be asked of the farmer.

In this situation, each worker still has two strategic alternatives: he can either support or not support the group action. What each worker can obtain, from either strategy, depends again upon what others do. But the contingencies relevant for his calculation of payoffs are different in this case. Each worker confronts three contingencies: (1) enough other workers (assume this number to be eight) participate that the group will win without

---

[4]We will reconsider nonself-enforcing schemes in Section IV of this chapter.
[5]The proportion needed for success is immaterial as long as the net group benefits are positive.

his help in the slowdown; (2) the support of others is just enough so that his support will make them prevail, but his lack of support will make them fail (i.e., exactly seven others support the slowdown); and (3) so many others defect from the slowdown that his contribution would be inefficacious (i.e., fewer than seven others support the slowdown).

The payoffs associated with each strategy depend upon the actions of others. These are represented in Table 3–2. The outcome is always either the supply or nonsupply of the additional wage. Notice that in this situation, there is no single strategy which is unconditionally best: best in each possible contingency. When eight or more others are expected to contribute to the slowdown, the worker prefers to defect and get the $5 by being a "free rider." Similarly, when fewer than seven others are expected to contribute, he prefers to defect and get nothing rather than lend his costly support to a losing cause. Only in the second contingency when he expects exactly seven others to contribute does he prefer to help in the slowdown. In that contingency, his participation would yield $4 rather than the $0 that he would get if he defected. Thus, in this situation, he cannot identify an unconditionally best strategy.

The nonexistence of an unconditionally best strategy choice in this case follows from the workers' engineering of a threshold for effective collective action.[6] In this case, the marginal cost sharing follows from the creation of an "all or nothing" contingency that defines the threshold for effective action, where each contributing individual makes the difference between the supply and nonsupply of the entire (or lumpy) collective goal. By restructuring the cost-sharing scheme, each worker can perceive that his contribution *may* furnish the particular share of the cost that would yield the entire bonus of $5.

But, of course, in such circumstances, each individual faces more than the contingency in which his contribution is productive. The other two contingencies in which he prefers not to contribute also confront him. Faced with these three contingencies then, how can the worker decide what to do? If he must act without sure knowledge of what the others will do, he must act with uncertainty as to the consequences of his behavior. He must choose between two alternatives. One involves the payoffs associated with his participation in the slowdown, as indicated in the first row of Table 3–2. The

Table 3–2   Returns to the Worker if Eight People Are Needed for Successful Slowdown

		Number of others contributing to the slowdown		
		8 or more	*7*	*fewer than 7*
INDIVIDUAL'S ALTERNATIVE STRATEGIES	Engage in slowdown	$4	$4	$-1
	Defect from group action	$5	$0	$0

[6]Here we have assumed the threshold to be beyond the range of any single individual's contributions.

other involves the payoffs associated with nonparticipation in the group effort (as given in the second row of that table).

If he is to choose rationally, he must have a preference order among these strategies. But the psychological assumptions of rational choice are insufficient to predict his preferences (and hence choices) in any situation involving no unconditionally better strategy. Considering conditionally optimal strategies points to a fundamental limitation on the applicability of the original set of psychological assumptions. An extension of the concept of rationality is needed to determine which strategy will be chosen and hence when marginal cost-sharing arrangements will induce the individual to support collective action.

II. ADDING TO THE RATIONALITY ASSUMPTION

Theorists don't agree on which assumptions should be added to the rationality assumptions to explain and predict behavior in contingent situations. At least three different assumptions have been advanced by political theorists. These may be referred to as (1) minimax, (2) maximin regret, and (3) expected value maximization. In choosing among them for the purpose of extending our analysis, we are interested in using the assumption that is the most closely descriptive of individual behavior in the political situations in question. However, it is still an open empirical question as to which is best in any situation. It is possible that in *some* situations, individuals maximize expected value, while in others they act in accordance with minimax or maximin regret. It is also possible (indeed in our opinion highly probable) that different individuals employ different behavioral rules. Unfortunately, not enough empirical and theoretical attention has been devoted to the problem to achieve any consensus.[7] However, the remainder of the book will deal almost exclusively with conclusions derived using expected value maximization. Since wide use is made of the other assumptions, we briefly examine each of the three possible additions to the basic rationality assumption.

Minimax Behavior

Consider again the decision situation faced by each of the farm workers represented in Table 3–2. The problem in explaining or predicting what constitutes rational behavior in that situation turns upon the fact that neither of his strategies is unconditionally preferred. His preferred strategic choice is contingent upon the action of the others. Under the first and third contingencies, he prefers to defect, but under his second contingency he prefers to engage in the slowdown. In choosing whether or not to slow down, individuals could choose *as if they expect the worst to happen.* Put one way, individuals could act conservatively by identifying the worst possible outcome that could befall them for each strategy and rank the strategies on that

---

[7]Recently, a number of experiments by Charles Plott and Michael E. Levine were conducted to gather data on precisely this point. See their "On Using the Agenda to Influence Group Decisions: Theory, Experiments and an Application," *Social Science Working Paper* No. 66, Nov. 74, Pasadena: California Institute of Technology.

basis. A person evaluating his options in this manner would choose the strategy associated with the least bad possibility. Such a person would maximize his "security level." Thus, minimax leads to the strategy that guaranteed the *highest minimum payoff.*

Suppose our farmworkers chose in accordance with the minimax assumption. Each would note that a strategy of contributing *could* result in a loss of $1. But the worst that could happen to a worker choosing not to slowdown would be that he would break even. Losing $1 is worse than breaking even. Thus, minimax would lead each not to contribute. The result: the slowdown would collapse, and collective action would fail.

Although the minimax assumption has a number of properties to recommend its use,[8] we believe that it does not lead to an accurate description of political behavior in situations of the sort sketched here. Afterall, if individuals conformed to the minimax assumption, they would *never* choose to contribute to a collective effort. Minimax leads to a withholding of support as long as there is a possibility of losing one's contribution.

If individuals always behaved this way, only groups in which some individuals valued the collective good more than the cost would succeed in getting voluntary supply of the good. For only in such cases could an individual be sure that he would be able to get some return for his contribution.

Clearly this assumption is too pessimistic. Individuals are willing to undertake *some* risks if returns are sufficiently high and/or sufficiently likely to follow as a result of their action. Some individuals may behave in a minimax fashion all of the time and all may do so some of the time, but surely not all do so all of the time.[9] When costs associated with the "worst" outcomes are particularily variable, and other aspects of one's payoffs (such as rewards accruing in the "best" of cases) are less subject to variation, we might expect minimax behavior to predominate. At other times, other forms of behavior may be more pronounced.

Maximin Regret

An alternative, but less pessimistic, assumption is the so-called *maximin regret assumption,* where individuals take into account not only the worst outcomes in each strategy but all possible outcomes. An individual choosing in a maximin regret fashion would evaluate each strategy in the following way. For each contingency (column) the maximum possible return is identified.

[8]Not the least of these are its "equilibrium" properties in purely competitive situations. The theory of games, developed by John Von Neumann and Oscar Morgenstarn are based on this assumption. But their theory is beyond the scope of this book. Interested readers are referred to the works indicated in the bibliographical note at the end of the Preface.

[9]Nevertheless, minimax behavior may help explain the difficulty in organizing groups for political action where it is prevalent. Moreover, a number of theorists have developed models of political processes based on this sort of calculation. So, for example, models of threats, bargaining, and international relations have been developed from a game theoretic perspective by Schelling and Rapoport. Other models of coalition formation, and the like, are often predicated on similar behavior. See Thomas C. Schelling, *The Strategy of Conflict,* New York: Oxford, 1960 and Anatol Rapoport, *Fights, Games, and Debates,* Ann Arbor: University of Michigan Press, 1960, for interesting examples of such applications.

Then the payoff associated with a given strategy in that column is subtracted from that maximum. The resultant number, either positive or zero, reflects how much one could fail to gain if the strategy in question were chosen and the contingency occurred. This "loss" or "regret" is one possible loss associated with the choice of the strategy in question. Other possible "losses" or "regrets" that could be suffered are computed by performing a similar operation in each column. The largest of these numbers represents the maximum possible "loss" or "regret" associated with the choice of the strategy in question. Each of these are viewed as possible sources of regret from choosing the strategy in question. The maximum of these is referred to as the strategy's *maximum possible regret number.* These numbers are computed for each of the strategies and that strategy with the smallest maximum possible regret number is chosen. In other words, the individual attempts to minimize his maximum possible regret at choosing a strategy.

Table 3–3 shows an application of the maximim regret assumption to the farmworker example. Consider the possible regret levels of each strategy. Begin with the strategy of supporting the collective action. In the first contingency (eight or more others participate): the strategy of supporting the slowdown yields a possible regret of $1 (the difference between the first column maximum of $5 and $4 which could be obtained by contributing). In the second column, contributing yields the best payoff in the column and thus a possible regret of zero. Were seven others to contribute, it would be the best possible strategy. Finally, contributing is associated with a regret of 1 (the loss of the $1 contribution) if fewer than seven others contribute. Thus *the maximum possible regret associated with contributing is $1.* The *strategy* of *not contributing,* however, has a *higher possible regret.* It has a possible regret of $0 in the first and third contingencies, but in the second it has a possible regret of $4. The high regret in the second stems from the fact that the defecting individual gets $0 when he could have obtained $4 by contributing. Therefore, the worker trying to minimize his maximum possible regret would, in this example, choose to contribute.

But just as the minimax assumption was posited to be too pessimistic to describe political behavior in general, it is relatively easy to make a *prima facia* case that the maximin regret assumption is too sanguine. *Under the maximin regret assumption an individual will always contribute as long as what he might gain is valued more than the contribution which is asked of him.*

Table 3–3   Maximin Regret Returns to the Worker if Eight People Are Needed for Successful Slowdown

			Number of others contributing to the slowdown		
			8 or more	*7*	*fewer than 7*
INDIVIDUAL'S ALTERNATIVE STRATEGIES	Engage	[Payoff] Regret	[$4] $1	[$4] $0	[$-1] $1
	Defect	[Payoff] Regret	[$5] $0	[$0] $4	[$0] $0

Given the history of failed collective enterprises of high value in which individuals have been asked for small amounts of support, it seems difficult to maintain that individuals generally behave in a maximin regret fashion. Once again, it is possible that this assumption is of general importance in some particular political situations or in some particular groups,[10] but as a general rule it does not seem promising. More specifically, we can imagine that when the most significant difference between alternatives is the "spread" between worst and best outcomes in various contingencies, maximin regret behavior might dominate. This may also be true for behavior that has a peculiarly salient "ethical" or "moral" dimension to it. But otherwise, we would expect that maximin regret would not be the general rule.

Maximizing Expected Value

Neither the minimax nor the maximin regret assumptions are very flexible. Neither allows for changes in an individual's choice as a function of the projected behavior of others. Both are essentially projections of a decision rule premised only on the possible payoffs facing the actor. An alternative analysis of the rational decision maker is available. If he knows the odds of each of the contingencies occurring, he may attempt to estimate the likely behavior of others and take that estimation into account in his decision. Were he to do this, he would be confronted with a set of contingencies, each of which has specific odds or probabilities attached to them. The payoffs associated with each strategy would resemble payoffs associated with a gamble or lottery. His choice of strategy would amount to a choice between different gambles.

If a rational individual attempts to incorporate the probabilities of each contingency occurring in his choice, how does he estimate the odds of the contingencies occurring, and, having arrived at probabilities, how does he rank the alternative strategies? As far as we are aware, there are few assumptions regarding how estimations of probabilities, or odds, are arrived at. But the second question has been dealt with by a rather simple set of assumptions. It is assumed that individuals who evaluate gambles, or alternatives involving specifiable risks, rank order the alternatives in terms of their "expected value," preferring that alternative associated with the maximum expected value. Although axiomatic treatment cannot be presented here, the main ideas can be laid out without much difficulty.

The first concept needing clarification for an appreciation of the expected utility maximization assumption is the concept of a gamble. A gamble is characterized by a set of possible outcomes, each of which has some *associated probability of being received.* A gamble (G) is a set of mutually exclusive and exhaustive outcomes ($O_1, O_2, \ldots, O_i, \ldots, O_n$) and associated probabilities ($p_1, p_2, \ldots, p_i, \ldots, p_n$). That is, one and only one of the

[10]See John A. Ferejohn and Morris P. Fiorina, "The Paradox of Not Voting: A Decision Theoretic Analysis," *American Political Science Review,* LXVIII, No. 2, June 1974, pp. 525–536, for a discussion of the preliminary "fit" of this assumption to American voting data. Note that maximin regret requires a far more restrictive set of assumptions than does the minimax assumption. For minimax purely ordinal properties of preferences suffice to explain the decisions.

outcomes must occur. Because the gamble involves mutually exclusive and exhaustive outcomes, the probabilities associated with the receipt of each of these outcomes add up to 1. That is: $\sum_i^n p_i = 1$. We can write a gamble involving n different possible outcomes as $G = (O_1 p_1, O_2 p_2, \ldots, O_n p_n)$.[11]

Gambles are the objects to be evaluated. If an individual is to evaluate the expected value of a gamble, he must consider not only his preferences regarding outcomes, but also the probabilities associated with receiving those outcomes. For example, assume Mr. J is offered two gambles: one with a chance to win a prize of \$20 or lose \$1, and another with a \$30 prize or a loss of \$1. Even though he prefers \$30 to \$20, as an expected value maximizer, Mr. J would not necessarily prefer the gamble with the \$30 prize. The probability of winning the prizes in the two gambles must be taken into account. If the odds of winning the \$30 is sufficiently smaller than the odds of winning the \$20, he will prefer the gamble with the smaller prize. Mr. J does this because he orders his preferences over gambles in terms of a *combination* of the payoffs and risks. Thus, the problem of evaluating gambles is reduced to the formal question of how payoffs and risks are combined. More specifically, it is assumed that the individual evaluates gambles by discounting each payoff by the probability of its receipt and then calculating the weighted sum of these "expected payoffs." For example, consider the gamble with the prize of \$20 and the possible loss of \$1. If these are the only two outcomes, let p_1 be the chance of losing \$1, and let p_{20} be the chance of gaining \$20. Then $p_1 + p_{20} = 1$, or the chance of getting \$20 is $1 - p_1$. If we designate Mr. J's value of \$20 as $V_j(20)$ and if we call his valuation of a \$1 loss $V_j(-1)$, then the weighted sum of these items can be used to represent Mr. J's valuation of the gamble, $V_j(G)$. Or

$$V_j(G) = V_j(20)(1 - p_1) + V_j(-1)p_1.$$

But this formulation underscores a difficulty. To compute a weighted sum of the values of the outcomes and the associated probabilities it is necessary that the individual evaluate the outcomes in terms of a *numerical scale*, or index. Indeed, expected value maximization must rely on a scale capable of multiplication by probability numbers. This requires more than the simple ordinality of preferences. The expected value of a gamble is then necessarily related to a numerical scale.[12] This scale is called a *utility* scale.

We might well consider what additional assumptions, regarding the psychology of choice, must be added to the notion of transitive preference and maximization so such a scale can be used.

[11]Note that with this notation a "sure bet" is a special form of a gamble, where all the probabilities, except the one associated with the sure bet outcome, are set equal to zero.

[12]Note that this utility scale needs to be more than ordinal. It must allow for interval numerical assignment to outcomes. Obviously the numbers instituting a utility scale must have specific properties. The psychological justification for the existence of a scale with these properties has led to numerous alternative formulations, all leading to similar (but not identical) scales. Construction of such a 'utility index' involves further psychological assumptions. To see why, c.f. R. Duncan Luce and Howard Raiffa, *Games and Decisions*, New York: Wiley, 1957, Chaps. 2 and 13. Note that these assumptions are implicitly required for two of the three candidates for the general solution of contingent choice problems.

Although most of the assumptions will not be discussed, the major building block of such a scale is easy to communicate and is usually referred to as *connectivity*. For illustrative purposes, assume a Mr. i prefers x to y to z. If all we assume is the transitivity of preference, any assignment of numbers to these three alternatives could serve as an (ordinal) utility scale as long as the number assigned to x (u_x) was higher than the number assigned to y (u_y), was higher than the number assigned to z (u_z).

But to use a scale for the evaluation of gambles, a stronger set of assumptions must be used. Such a scale could be constructed in the following manner. Let Mr. i choose between two options: first, a gamble involving x and z as equally probable prizes, and second, the certainty of y. First note that the gamble with a fifty-fifty chance of x and z would seem to naturally fall "midway" between x and z. Similarly, the gamble involving a three out of four chance to get x rather than z, would seem to fall naturally three-fourths of the way toward x from z. Suppose the individual prefers y, to the fifty-fifty chance of x or z (or to the midpoint). Clearly, the individual's valuation of y should be placed closer to his valuation of x than to his valuation of z. If the individual prefers the certainty of y to the gamble between x and z, when x is assured with a probability of three-fourths, it seems natural to say that the utility number of y should be more than three-fourths of the way from the utility number of z to the utility number associated with x. In general, Mr. i can be faced with alternative gambles between x and z (differing in the probability of receiving x) until he finds himself indifferent between y and a particular gamble such that x is to be received with a specified probability p^*. A utility scale can then be constructed that would assign x some u_x, z some u_z ($u_z < u_x$), and would assign u_y such that it was p^* of the way from u_z to u_x. Or, if u_z is arbitrarily assigned a value of 0, and u_x is assigned a value of 1, then u_y is p^*.

The expected value of a gamble is then calculable as follows. Each outcome in the gamble is assigned its utility number. Then each such number is multiplied by the probability that the outcome will occur. The sum of these products is the expected value of the gamble. Thus, if u_1 is the utility number for the ith outcome in the gamble $G = (O_1 p_1, O_2 p_2, \ldots, O_i p_i, \ldots, O_n p_n)$ then the expected value of the gamble is $EV(G) = u_1 p_1 + u_2 p_2 + \ldots + u_i p_i + \ldots + u_n p_n$. In a situation involving a number of gambles as potential choices, the expected value maximizer would compute such a sum for each gamble. He would choose that gamble associated with the highest expected value.

This approach directs our attention to the subjective probability estimations of the individuals. This is in juxtaposition with the previous two sets of assumptions. These differences could give us some "intuitive expectations" as to when individuals are likely to behave in accordance with any of the assumptions. For example, if no knowledge of the "likelihoods" of the contingencies is available, then the maximin regret and minimax hypotheses appear more credible. Further, assuming no knowledge of probabilities is attainable, if differences between the alternatives are primarily those things that would happen if the worst of all possible worlds came to pass, then minimax, rather than maximin regret, would seem to be called for. That is, in situations where one is specifically trying to "establish a security level" (e.g., the establishment of an insurance, or guarantee, etc.), minimax would conceivably have considerable predictive power.[13] On the other hand, where probabilities can meaningfully be estimated, expected value notions make considerable sense. Of course, within such situations, the expected value hypothesis allows for a greater variety of behavior than the other candidates for the job. It is conceivable, for example, that even with similar evaluation of the payoffs, some individuals in a particular situation will act one way and others will act another way because they have differing expectations regarding the likelihood of each contingency occurring. That is, they estimate the probabilities differently. Compared to the other two assumptions, expected value allows for a greater variety of predicted behavior, hence a narrower class of "falsifying behavior," and the hypothesis is harder to test.

III. EXPECTED VALUE MAXIMIZATION AND COLLECTIVE ACTION

Returning to the example of the slowdown, we can reformulate the worker's alternatives as gambles. One of the worker's options is to choose that gamble associated with the strategy of contributing to the slowdown. The other option is the gamble associated with his defection from the collective effort. In either case, his probability of receiving the benefits of a successful slowdown are dependent on the actions of the other workers. The success of the slowdown depends on both his action and the action of the others.

More specifically, let us call the probability that eight or more others contribute to the slowdown p_1; the probability that seven others make such contributions p_2; and the probability that fewer than seven others make such contributions p_3. Then let $U(\$5)$ be his utility valuation of the $5 outcome, $U(\$4)$ his valuation of the $4 outcome, and so on.

Each of his two strategies can be characterized as gambles. The strategy of slowing down can be called gamble 1, or G_1.[14]

$$G_1 = \{U(\$5 - \$1)P_1, \ U(\$5 - \$1)P_2, \ U(-\$1)P_3\}$$

Similarly G_2 represents the gamble associated with not slowing down.

$$G_2 = \{U(\$5)P_1, \ U(\$0)P_2, \ U(\$0)P_3\}$$

[13]See John Rawls, *A Theory of Justice,* Cambridge: Harvard, 1971, pp. 154–155, and William Fellner, *Probability & Profit,* Homewood, Ill.: Irwin, 1965, pp. 140–142.

[14]This representation (and that of maximin regret) requires more than normal utility scales for its conclusions. Utility numbers cannot be used to represent the *differences* in utility numbers without further assumptions. For further discussion of this, see Luce and Raiffa, op. cit., Chap. 2. Here we assume: $u(\$5) - u(\$1) = u(\$5 - \$1) = u(\$4)$, or the utility of monetary differences is the utility difference between payoffs. This amounts to "constant marginal valuation of money," an assumption sometimes utilized in standard monetary economics. For an examination of the effect of variable marginal utility of money, see Milton Friedman and L. J. Savage, "The Utility Analysis of Choices Involving Risk," *The Journal of Political Economy,* LVI, Aug. 1948, pp. 279–304.

We can calculate the expected value of each gamble directly as:

$$EV(G_1) = U(\$5 - \$1)P_1 + U(\$5 - \$1)P_2 + U(-\$1)P_3 \quad (3.1)$$

$$EV(G_2) = U(\$5)P_1 + U(\$0)P_2 + U(\$0)P_3 \quad (3.2)$$

Therefore, an expected value maximizer would be willing to contribute only if $EV(G_1)$ were greater than $EV(G_2)$. With this in mind, we can compute the general conditions that such an individual would find it worthwhile choosing to help in the slowdown.

From equations 3.1 and 3.2, setting $U(\$0)$ as the arbitrary zero point on his utility scale (i.e. the status quo), this condition becomes: $U(\$5)$ $(P_1 + P_2) - U(\$1)(P_1 + P_2 + P_3) > U(\$5)P_1$. But this can be simplified by noting that $P_1 + P_2 + P_3 = 1$, by cancelling like terms on either side of the inequality and rearranging terms to yield:

$$U(\$5)P_2 > U(\$1) \quad (3.3)$$

But this, the condition for contributing, is directly interpretable. P_2, after all, is the probability that the individual's donation is absolutely necessary for the attainment of the objective, and is sufficient (given the behavior of others) for the success of the enterprise. P_2, therefore, is the probability of making a difference for the attainment of the bonus. It follows that $U(\$5)$ P_2 is the expected value of making a difference. $U(\$1)$ is the cost of getting this. Thus the expected value of making a difference must be greater than the individual's cost of contributing to the collective action.

In the example of the farmworkers, assuming money is a good index for the farmworker's preferences $[U(\$5) = 5$ and $U(\$1) = 1]$ we can be more specific. In this case, from (3.3), the inequality becomes $5P_2 > 1$. Thus the probability of making a difference must be greater than the ratio of costs to benefits (divide both sides of the inequality by 5) or $P_2 > 1/5$.[15] Only in this case will the individual find it worthwhile to contribute to the collective effort. He must feel that the probability of making a difference, or the chance that precisely seven others will help in the slowdown, is greater than one-fifth or he will not contribute.

What was shown for the farmworker example can be generalized to all political action decisions. *If the individual is to be motivated to donate to a political cause strictly by his evaluation of the collective benefits, the expected value of the difference he can make must be greater than the cost he must bear to make that difference.* That is, the inequality (3.3) must hold.[16]

It should be clear that the expected value assumption is neither overly optimistic nor overly pessimistic regarding individual inclinations to contribute. In this sense it is different from the minimax and maximin regret assumptions. Rather, the expected behavior of others becomes an important

[15]Again, ratios of utility numbers are not meaningful without the additional assumptions used.

[16]This analysis parallels the authors', "I Get by with a Little Help from My Friends," *World Politics*, XXIII, No. 1, Oct. 1970, pp. 104–120.

factor in determining any individual's decision. If someone is pessimistic regarding the behavior of others, he may feel that the group just won't be capable of sufficient contributions to succeed, and so he won't contribute. Similarly, if someone is sanguine regarding others' actions, he may view a contribution as redundant. Only if a person places a sufficiently high probability estimation on the likelihood that *his* contribution can make a difference will he have an incentive to contribute.

This focus on the chance to make a difference lets us analyze the major problem of obtaining political participation or contributions. If collective action is to be forthcoming at an effective level among the workers, we assumed eight out of the ten individuals had to be motivated to participate. If they are expected value maximizers, eight of the workers each must believe that there is greater than a one-fifth chance of precisely seven others supporting the slowdown.[17] Each of the eight must reach this conclusion. This requirement can be generalized as political laws:

1. *Successful political action based solely on the individuals' incentives to obtain the collectively supplied good requires marginal cost sharing, and*
2. *Successful marginal cost sharing requires that a sufficient number of individuals each believe that the probability that their contribution will make the difference in obtaining the collective good is greater than the ratio of their cost to benefit.*

Although such complementary patterns of mutual expectations among group members are a general requirement for successful voluntary action, such patterns cannot be expected to spring up spontaneously. These patterns are not likely, especially in groups with neither prior organizational arrangements nor common experiences.

Therefore, we conclude:

An agreement to share the marginal cost of a collective good will not by itself be sufficient to induce individuals to live up to that agreement.

A *marginal cost-sharing* scheme may be *necessary* for the successful supply of collective goods, but *it is not, by itself, sufficient*. Without further organizing, the coordination of expectations (or complementary pattern of expectations) needed to motivate contributions will be absent. A group that relies on the collective good itself as the sole incentive for marginal cost sharing will fail to supply itself with the collective good in question.[18]

[17]Of course, it may be that there is no precisely perceived threshold on the part of any individual. In such a case, the range over which the threshold varies can be interpreted as a set of mutually exclusive possibilities with associated probabilities. In such a case, each possibility represents another contingency under which the individual's contribution could "make the difference" and the reasoning is analogous.

[18]An alternative perspective on the outcome of prisoner dilemma games has been put forward by a number of theorists, based on more complex assumptions. The reader should examine Nigel Howard, *Paradoxes of Rationality: Theory of Metagames and Political Behavior*, Cambridge, Mass: M.I.T. Press, 1971; and Michael Taylor, *Anarchy and Cooperation*, New York: John Wiley, 1976. These works develop a theoretical but controversial perspective from which one can expect that cooperation on a purely voluntary basis can lead to an escape from the prisoners' dilemma.

IV. OVERCOMING THE BARRIER TO PARTICIPATION: SUPPLYING EXCLUDABLE INCENTIVES

The question of successful political organization has now become: How can a marginal cost-sharing scheme be made effective? The answer to that question is two-fold.

The first step is to supplement the incentives that the collective good itself gives individuals: to motivate people with privately supplied benefits and supply incentives on a selective, or excludable basis. People are unlikely to be sufficiently motivated by incentives that involve collectively supplied benefits and privately incurred costs. This was a major argument of Olson in *The Logic of Collective Action.* The supplementary incentives may be either (positive) rewards, for participation in the collective effort, or (negative) punishments, for nonparticipation. But the incentives must be individualized, and hence must be excludable, if we are to break out of the problem of suboptimal supply tied to collective goods. The incentives can even be post-facto reimbursement (as in the farmworker case, where the workers all pool their wages). But in each situation, the individual must be able to be treated differently if he donates or if he refuses to donate to the collective project.

Given the high value of some collective goods, potential recipients often value the establishment of a system of excludable incentives to overcome this barrier to effective political action. Since everyone could benefit by such incentives, there could well be unanimous acceptance of such a system. Indeed, individuals might even accept a system in which noncontributors were threatened with dire consequences and punished. In other words, *rational individuals will often need to be, and agree to be, forced to do what they wish to do anyhow.* An interesting illustration of this "paradox" is reported by Olson:

> Thus there is a paradoxical contrast between the extremely low participation in labor unions and the overwhelming support that workers give to measures that will force them to support a union. *Over 90 percent will not attend meetings or participate in union affairs; yet over 90 percent will vote to force themselves to belong to the union and make considerable dues payments to it.* An interesting study by Hjalmer Rosen and R. A. Hudson Rosen illustrates this paradox well.[19] The Rosens conducted an opinion survey of District 9 of the International Association of Machinists and found many workers who told them that, since fines for absences from union meeting had been discontinued, attendance had dropped, as one member put it, "something awful." There was more dissatisfaction among the members over the poor attendance than on any other point covered in the extensive survey; only 29% were satisfied with the attendance at meetings. The Rosens inferred from this that the members were probably inconsistent. "If the rank and file feel that members should attend meetings and are dissatisfied when they don't, why don't they correct the situation by all going to the meetings? The condition they are dissatisfied with is certainly in their power to change."[20]

[19]Hjalmer Rosen and R. A. Hudson Rosen, *The Union Member Speaks,* Englewood Cliffs, N.J.: Prentice-Hall, 1955, as cited in Olson, *op. cit.*
[20]Rosen and Rosen, op. cit., pp. 82–83, as cited in Olson.

In fact, the workers were not inconsistent: their actions and attitudes were a model of rationality when they wished that everyone would attend meetings and failed to attend themselves. For if a strong union is in the members' interest, they will presumably be better off if the attendance is high, but (when the fines for failure to attend meetings are not in effect) an individual worker has no economic incentive to attend a meeting. He will get the benefits of the union's achievements whether he attends meetings or not and will probably not by himself be able to add noticeably to those achievements.[21]

As indicated, force isn't the only possible incentive. But some selective incentive is usually needed.

Thus, how to overcome the "paradox of nonparticipation" can involve the introduction of selective incentives. But remember, we have already shown that these selective incentives are not *logically* necessary. One other possibility remains. If individuals are expected value maximizers, and if they develop just the proper expectations regarding the behavior of others, they will also choose to contribute or participate. Such a situation is, however, very tenuous, and is likely to occur only when there is some manipulation of the people's expectations in the prescribed manner. Furthermore, it is not likely that such manipulation can be maintained over long periods of time, nor that it could sustain very costly collective action. Rather, we would expect that sustained and costly collective efforts will require more "institutionalized" systems of incentives.

Regardless of how resources are secured for the group effort, some important questions remain. For example, where do these systems of incentives come from in a group of rational individuals? If most groups will need to have excludable incentives, what consequences will this have on the structure of politics within the group? Furthermore, even if resources can be raised through the application of excludable incentives, why should these resources get ploughed back into the benefits that originally concerned the group members? Consider a taxer, threatening people for nonpayment of a tax? Why should the moneys that are being collected be spent on collective goods rather than on personal pleasure yachts, private castles, etc? These are some of the questions we deal with in the next chapter.

V. FOR FURTHER READING

A fuller, and yet elementary presentation of cardinal utility scales and expected value behavior is given in John Von Neumann and Oskar Morgenstern, *Theory of Games and Economic Behavior,* 3rd ed. (New York: Wiley, 1953), pp. 15–30; Duncan Luce and Howard Raiffa, *Games and Decisions* (c.f. footnote 12) and Anatol Rapoport, *Two Person Game Theory* Ann Arbor: Univ. Of Michigan, 1970. A useful reader on the subject has been edited: Page, *Utility Theory: A Book of Readings,* New York: Wiley, 1968.

---

[21]Mancur Olson, *op. cit.,* p. 86. Italics in the original.

CHAPTER FOUR

POLITICAL ORGANIZING
AND
POLITICAL ENTREPRENEURS

By now the reader should be convinced that many political problems are problems stemming from the calculations of rational, self-interested individuals attempting to supply themselves with collective goods. Collective goods alone are an insufficient basis for effective collective action. Other incentives are needed to motivate individuals. These incentives must either be selective incentives, or a belief that the individual's effort could be crucial in supplying the good in question.

But, these incentives are costly. Selective incentives can be rewards to those who help supply the good, or punishments to those who don't. Using the farmworker example, a beer party for workers who pool their wages would be a positive selective incentive (or reward). Slashing the tires of workers who did not participate in the slowdown would be a negative selective incentive (or punishment). Making the worker feel his contribution was needed, requires manipulation and communication. All of these incentives are costly to supply: beer costs money—there are laws against slashing tires. If individuals are rational and self interested why would someone bear the costs of providing these incentives?[1]

[1] On rare occasions an incentive system may be relatively costless. In geographically compact, static societies, in which the same few collective goods require provision over time, costs may be minimal. Traditions might have evolved which serve to provide the incentives necessary to overcome suboptimality. For example tradition might fix the expected size and type of each individual's contribution to any group effort. This would serve to coordinate group expectations and lead to a sense of individual efficacy in that each individual came to think of his contribution as essential. The maintenance of such a system could be relatively costless to the extent that individuals continued, in the light of repeated success, to believe the traditions effective. Often, as an added "costless" incentive, the traditions may identify rewards or punishment in the afterlife, or from the "gods" in this life to those who help or fail to support the group effort. But in general, in any population subject to change (in a modern urban setting for example) where a changing variety of collective goods are needed over time, substantial costs will be required to maintain an ongoing and flexible system of incentives.

If incentives are not supplied, the group will fail to achieve optimal levels of the good. This failure: suboptimality, implies than an expenditure by the group could yield a benefit that would be greater than the cost incurred. (See Chap. 3.) The benefits of moving toward optimality might be sufficiently great to make them all better off even if they paid for an incentive system. Thus, if someone were willing to expend the efforts necessary to provide an incentive system and thereby organize the group, conceivably he could be subsidized by the group for his efforts. Such an individual could get an extra reward for his efforts and thereby be given an incentive to organize the group for the effective supply of the good. Notice that *everyone* could be better off under this arrangement. As long as group benefits are greater than the organizing costs plus the costs of the good, there is a surplus that could be used to reward the organizer.

To illustrate, consider again the farmworker example of Chapter 4. Each worker stood to gain $4 by a successful slowdown if he contributed. Suppose that for $2 from each of them, one of the workers offered to talk to all of the others on behalf of the slowdown, give a beer party for all who went along, and slash the tires of those who didn't.[2] If they all paid, they could each still end up with $2 profit, plus a beer party (assuming that the organizing tactics worked) and the organizer might more than cover his costs.

The job just described as so crucial in supplying collective goods is characteristically the job of political leaders. Political leaders *can organize groups* using a variety of incentives, supply the goods, make a profit and yet leave everyone better off. But the fact that political organizers *can* be rewarded, and still leave everyone better off, does not insure that everyone *will* be better off if an organizer sets up an incentive system. Indeed, because the organizer usually must raise resources using excludable incentives separated from the collective good, there is a chance that people will give resources to an enterprising organizer, yet fail to get collective goods in return. The world has a long history of tyrannts who supplied few, or no positively valued collective goods. Which factors lead to responsible leadership? How do political contexts and motivational patterns combine to allow one to predict the behavior of political leaders? To develop an answer to this question, this chapter examines the nature of political leadership in a variety of political contexts. Differing concerns of rational leaders will be shown to follow from different contextual settings.

I. ENTREPRENEURIAL LEADERS

Entrepreneurship has long been studied in economics and assumptions about entrepreneurial motivations and functions play an important role in economic theory. Remarkably, economists have failed to agree upon a common definition of entrepreneurship. Some emphasize motivation while oth-

---

[2]The point does not require that the entrepreneurial leader ask for, or receive monetary benefits.

ers cite activity as the defining characteristic. One major scholar in the field defines entrepreneurship in terms of preferences that lead to profit maximizing behavior.[3] Others have emphasized the function, or job aspect, as the definitive aspect of entrepreneurship. Samuelson, for example, views the entrepreneur as an innovator.[4] Joseph Schumpeter's characterization of the entrepreneurial role is most useful (from our perspective):

> ... the function of entrepreneurs is to reform or revolutionize the pattern of production by exploiting an invention or, more generally, an untried technological possibility for producing a new commodity or producing an old one in a new way, by opening up a new source of supply of materials or a new outlet for products, by reorganizing an industry and so on ... To undertake such new things is difficult and constitutes a distinct economic function, first, because they lie outside of the routine tasks which everybody understands and, secondly, because the environment resists in many ways that vary, according to social conditions, from simple refusal either to finance or to buy a new thing, to physical attack on the man who tries to produce it. To act with confidence beyond the range of familiar beacons and to overcome that resistance requires aptitudes that are present in only a small fraction of the population and that define the entrepreneurial type as well as the entrepreneurial function. This function does not essentially consist in either inventing anything or otherwise creating conditions which the enterprise exploits. It consists in getting the things done.[5]

The conclusions in Chaps. 2 and 3 indicate that if groups are to achieve their collective interests and overcome suboptimality, they must accomplish this task. Someone must bear the initial costs of supplying incentives to induce contributions from group members. What is needed is an investor who innovates and collects the resources necessary to meet the group's needs. Because this task so closely resembles the job of the traditional economic entrepreneur, we refer to any individual performing this function as a *political entrepreneur*. Explicitly:

> *A political entrepreneur is an individual who invests his own time or other resources to coordinate and combine other factors of production to supply collective goods.*

In doing this the entrepreneur, in general, will have to obtain resources from others and enter into exchanges with them. It will be costly to supply

[3]See Tibor Scitovsky, *Welfare and Competition,* Homewood, Ill.: Irwin, revised ed., 1971, pp. 149–154, for a discussion of "in what sense and under what conditions the maximization of the entrepreneur's satisfaction coincides with the maximization of his profit."

[4]Paul A. Samuelson, *Economics: An Introductory Analysis,* 6th ed., New York: McGraw-Hill, 1964, pp. 602–3.

[5]Joseph A. Schumpeter, *Capitalism, Socialism and Democracy,* 3rd ed., New York: Harper and Row, 1950, p. 132. Note that these last two aspects of the entrepreneur can be combined. In Alfred W. Stonier and Douglas C. Hague, *A Textbook of Economic Theory,* New York: Wiley, 1953, the entrepreneur is described as "the one person in the firm who hires factors of production and that his decisions are always based on an attempt to maximize profits. His chief aim is to avoid losing money. It is clear, therefore, that the entrepreneur is a special type of factor of production. He is the only factor of reproduction whose duty it is to combine and organize other factors of production."

the incentives that he can use in his exchanges. As important as his job is, it will also be difficult and costly. Why, then, would a rational individual ever make such an investment of time, energy, and resources? It should be clear where these gains might come from. To overcome suboptimality the members must support the collection of resources. And the collection and pooling of resources controlled by the entrepreneur opens the possibility of self enrichment. Successfully overcoming of suboptimality also generates value for the group. In addition to these group and personal gains, there are a variety of gains to be had from entrepreneurial activity which satisfies a group's needs: honor, power, praise, fame, etc.

Put this way, the role of a political leader can be viewed as a job, much like any other. As George Washington Plunkitt put it, "Politics is as much a regular business as the grocery or the dry-goods or the drug business."[6] We would expect aspiring political leaders to evaluate their possible careers in terms of what they can get out of it, just as they would any other job. But the task facing the political entrepreneur is more complex than that facing the merchant. The merchant, to prosper, need only buy cheap and sell dear. The political entrepreneur must balance a complex set of incentives in his business. He must tax. He must reward. He must manipulate information to co-ordinate expectations. And in doing so he must raise enough to cover his cost and adequately reward his efforts.

Since entrepreneurs *can* gain rewards for themselves there is room for purely instrumental leadership. That is, political organizations may be founded less for the realization of group benefits than for the realization of rewards for the entrepreneur. In the words of Bertrand Russell:

> In every organization there are two purposes: one, the ostensible purpose for which the organization exists; the other, the increase in the power of its officials. This second purpose is very likely to make a stronger appeal to the officials concerned than the general public purpose that they are expected to serve.[7]

Thus, while we must wonder what motivates a rational individual to set up an organization purportedly to supply collective goods, we must also wonder what motivates him to pay continued attention to the public purpose of the organization. What keeps an entrepreneur responsive to his "clients"?

In economics the question need never be asked. If the business person stops manufacturing a desirable product, the customers stop buying. But the political leader can set up incentives *divorced* from the collective good. Hence raising revenue can be separated from supplying the collective good. Thus, we may ask why such a leader would need bother supplying the collective good at all and what conditions are conducive to responsible leadership?

[6]W. L. Riordan, *Plunkitt of Tammany Hall,* New York: Dutton, p. 19.

[7]Bertrand Russell, "Symptoms of Orwell's 1984," in B. Russell, *Portraits from Memory and Other Essays,* 202–210, London: George Allen & Unwin, p. 205 as quoted and cited in Thomas S. Szasz, *Law Liberty, and Psychiatry,* New York: Macmillan, 1963, p. 79.

Entrepreneurial Competition

Political entrepreneurs and economic entrepreneurs differ in the tools they must employ, and in the manipulations they must perform. They perform tasks that are different in an important way. If a consumer does not like the produce at a grocer's shop, he can buy at a different shop. But the supply of collective goods often does not allow for this sort of choice. If a collective good is supplied to one member of a group, it is supplied to all. And if one does not like the types of goods supplied, one generally can't just switch to another supplier.

To illustrate, suppose there were two possible uses for a piece of public land in the center of a city: a public park or a parking lot. Use of the land as a park precludes its use as a parking lot and vice versa. If some individuals want a park and some want the lot, one group will be dissatisfied no matter what is done. Now if a particular politician must make the decision, he must consider the dissatisfied group. They will view his program as undesirable. Indeed, on this basis they could view his removal and a change in his program *as a valuable collective good. Some other aspiring political entrepreneur could use that group and their desire for change as a base for organizing his own political apparatus.* The point can be made more generally:

> *Differences in preferences among collective good recipients lead to attempts to supply substitute collective goods.*

Since often, as in this example, *both* goods cannot be provided, competition is set up between the extant entrepreneur and the aspiring entrepreneur for control of the programs. Only one side can be victorious and the entrepreneur can find himself in a contest with an opponent bent on displacing him from his role.[8]

But the conflict need not be restricted to the question of which of two substitute collective goods to supply. The struggle can center on other questions (e.g., the general responsiveness of the leadership to the group's interests). Competition, therefore, is one means by which the group may be able to keep leaders from straying too far from their collective interests in the use of the resources raised by noncollective incentives.

However, we cannot expect too much from competition over political leadership positions. After all, an aspiring competitor's task is similar to the original political entrepreneur's task. The competitor has available only the same incentives to get resources as the original leader. Of course, his program, will usually involve a different resource base, but being a political leader himself he has analogous opportunities to reward himself.

---

[8]Other political solutions are possible, of course. People can leave the area or the political unit, and thereby remove themselves from the undesired programs by exodus or secession. Although secession is a logical possibility, in situations where there is a great deal of fixed investment which can't easily be parcelled out to the seceding groups, we would expect secession to be a rare occurrence. Indeed, it appears that only in relatively primitive societies is secession a normal form of political competition. See Lucy Mair, *Primitive Government* and I. Schapera, *Government and Politics in Tribal Societies,* New York: Schocken, 1967. A more theoretical work which deals with the alternatives to opposition is Albert O. Hirschman's *Exit, Voice and Loyalty,* Cambridge: Harvard University Press, 1970.

Differences between political and economic competition are critical for the understanding and analysis of the incentive structure facing the political entrepreneur. In economic competition, one competes for shares of the market. In politics, one competes to drive one's opponent out of business. In the words of one professional public-relations man specializing in political work:

> If you launch a campaign for a new car, your client doesn't expect you to lead the field necessarily in the first year, or even in the tenth year. If you're in third, fourth, or fifth place, that's good enough; you're still *one of the big five!* But in politics they don't pay off for PLACE OR SHOW! You have to win, if you want to stay in business.[9]

Displacement is the form political competition takes because political leaders are involved in the provision of nondivisible goods—goods that do not require increased supply to realize increased consumption.[10] This leads to the development of "natural monopolies" or situations where the established supplier is in a favored position to supply further services to the same constituent, thus preventing competition over "market shares."[11]

The political entrepreneur is in a career where opponents are continually looking to displace him and capture the rewards of his office. The political leader's job, therefore, has an acute element of risk. The way in which political entrepreneurs use their resources to cope with this risk is a major determinant of the political patterns of a system.

II. ENTREPRENEURIAL BEHAVIOR IN VARYING CONTEXTS

Political entrepreneurship has been identified as a job. As in all jobs, the rational worker can be expected to try to get as much as possible out of his work. Two factors affect what the entrepreneur can expect from his activity: the source of the rewards of office, and the risk associated with getting these rewards due to potential oppositions.

Assume that entrepreneurs evaluate their returns in an expected value fashion.[12] Thus, they evaluate their options as gambles with one eye on the rewards and with the other on the probabilities of obtaining them. Realistically, the political leader must often look beyond his current job. After all, he eventually will leave his position. Therefore, he would take into account and attempt to affect the rewards (or punishments) that would come his way

[9]Clem Whitaker in an address before the Los Angeles Area Chapter of the Public Relations Society of America, July 13, 1948, as quoted in Stanley Kelley, Jr. *Professional Public Relations and Political Power*, Baltimore: Hopkins, 1956, p. 46. In a system of proportional representation, of course, "winning" isn't everything. On the other hand, in those systems the question is of winning is usually delayed until legislative decisions are reached.

[10]See Chap. 3, pp. 32–35.

[11]For a fuller discussion of this point, see Norman Frohlich, Joe A. Oppenheimer, and Oran Young, *Political Leadership and Collective Goods*, Princeton: Princeton University Press, 1971, pp. 69–72.

[12]See Chap. 4, pp. 58–64.

were he to move into another role. Such a change of roles could result in a more attractive position, or to a far worse one. Algebraically, the leader is posited to maximize

$$U(L)P(L) + U(D)P[1 - P(L)],$$

where $U(L)$ represents the value of holding the entrepreneurial role, $P(L)$ the probability of holding the role, and $U(D)$ the rewards, or punishments associated with other roles to which he might move.

Immediately, this expression leads us to a binary distinction among all political situations. On the one hand are leadership positions which can be supported with sufficient rewards [U(L)] to make the position attractive to would-be leaders and those situations in which such a level of rewards is not sustainable. If individuals are expected value maximizers, and if most politicians are basically self-interested, competition will be stiffer for positions that are well rewarded. And if competition is required to insure responsiveness to a constituency, actions of political leaders should not be as "constituency oriented" or as subject to the demands of the constituency when the political leader does not stand to suffer by losing his position. Indeed, some political theorists have looked to personal ambitions as the necessary link to responsiveness by the political leader in a democracy:

> To slight the role of ambition in politics, then, or to treat it as a human failing to be supressed, is to miss the central function of ambition in political systems. A political system unable to kindle ambitions for office is as much in danger of breaking down as one unable to restrain ambitions. Representative government, above all, depends on a supply of men so driven; the desire for election and, more important, for re-election becomes the electorate's restraint upon its public officials. No more irresponsible government is imaginable than one of high-minded men unconcerned for their political futures.[13]

If ambition is to be tied to political responsiveness, rewards must be large enough to attract individuals to the job. Kenneth Prewitt has found that there are many jobs in politics, at least in local politics in the United States, that do not offer sufficient rewards to attract competitors. Further, he found that the individuals who were engaged as political leaders in such jobs did not feel themselves bound by the electorate that "put them in office." Where "officeholders simply conclude that the obligations of office exceed the rewards. . . . [B]oth the choosers and the chosen come to think of movement into and out of political office as being regulated by self-selection and self-elimination patterns rather than by electoral challenges."[14] In such situations, members of city councils vote more frequently against perceived majority opinion, perform fewer services for constituents, activate fewer groups and constituents in connection with policy making,

---

[13]Joseph A. Schlesinger, *Ambition and Politics,* Chicago: Rand McNally, 1966, p. 2, as cited and quoted in Kenneth Prewitt, "Political Ambitions, Volunteerism, and Electoral Accountability," American *Political Science Review,* LXIV, No. 1, March, 1970, p. 7.

[14]Prewitt, *op. cit.,* p. 10.

etc.[15] Finally, those who are active in politics as leaders don't stay with the job very long. "About one-fifth will be planning to retire voluntarily at the end of the present term and another 30 to 50 percent will be planning to retire after only one more term."[16] Conceivably many of these individuals undertake political activity largely or even solely in order to increase the values they can expect from the roles they will occupy upon leaving the political arena. Many lawyers and business executives engage in political activity for the contacts, increased business, and positive publicity for their corporations, which are expected to follow from their actions. What a far cry this is from the picture we paint of the risks which might follow from electoral defeat.

If political defeat is to be meaningful, it is presumably because the incumbent wants to keep the position and the associated rewards. If $U(L)$ is not large, individuals will be motivated to engage in political activity for the rewards they can obtain when they go back to their *other* careers (i.e., $U(D)$). How different from the small town political role studied by Prewitt is the role of the American member of Congress! "It seems fair to characterize the modern Congress as an assembly of professional politicians spinning out political careers. The jobs offer good pay and high prestige. There is no want of applicants. Successful pursuit of a career requires continual re-election."[17] In these sorts of situations, political entrepreneurs are usually more interested in $U(L)$ than in $U(D)$.[18]

In most important roles in established organizations, political entrepreneurs face opponents intent upon gaining the leaders' jobs. Madam Nhu, sister-in law of a former president of South Vietnam, remarked: "There's always going to be an opposition. If we take these people in, there will be another opposition springing up. . . ." An aide identified why this was the case." . . . it's a matter of others wanting to take our place. . . ."[19] Therefore, he will constantly be faced with the problem of how to invest his factors of production to increase his expected returns; should he invest to increase the size of his rewards or to increase his security?

This dual concern of increasing one's chance of staying in office and of increasing one's rewards from office manifests itself in different ways in differing political contexts. For example, when rewards of office are relatively fixed, a political leader usually will find it advantageous to concentrate his next investment on holding on to office. On the other hand, if the

[15]Prewitt, *op. cit.*, p. 11
[16]Prewitt, *op. cit.*, p. 10.
[17]David R. Mayhew, *Congress: The Electoral Connection*, New Haven: Yale, 1974, pp. 14–15.
[18]From time to time, however, politicians may have greatly increased interest in $U(D)$ [1-$P(L)$]. For example, toward the end of their tenure, Spiro Agnew and Richard Nixon, were both concerned almost exclusively with what would befall them upon leaving office. But even more extreme is the entrepreneur who specializes in leaving office. Riordan, *op. cit.* pp. 57–64 gives the example of political organizations ("democracies") founded solely to frighten Tammany Hall into buying out the founders with high paying patronage jobs. Such sham opposition entrepreneurs are presumably interested only in the rewards they can extract for leaving the competition as is evidenced by the way in which they dissolve their organizations immediately upon being bought out.
[19]Robert Shaplen, *The Lost Revolution*, New York: Harper and Row, 1966, p. 160.

entrepreneur sees little possibility of changing his security, he will specialize in increasing his rewards. In general, of course, political enterpreneurs must spread their investments over both of these factors. Yet there is a great deal of variation in the context of political activity. And these variations affect the incentives and returns that face the entrepreneur. Even if politicians always maximized expected value, their manifest behavior would vary as a function of the differing incentive systems inherent in different political contexts. For example, we would expect a materialistic maximizer who is a king, or despot, to behave differently from one who is an elected official. After all, their incentives differ. Yet differing incentives may make it appear that there are great differences in the motivations and values of political entrepreneurs.[20] Given the need to win in politics, the rules of political competition are clearly a relevant variable in the explanation of leadership behavior. These rules will have profound effects on the incentives leaders face. Let us begin, then, by contrasting the incentive structure of elected (as contrasted to non-elected) leadership. To maximize our leverage from the examination of rules, we begin by assuming all leaders are similarly motivated. In particular, until Section III of this Chapter, we assume leaders are primarily self-oriented.

Electoral versus Despotic Contexts

In an electoral context, the need to win translates via the constitutional, or electoral, rules into something rather concrete and definable. If there are only two competitors, for example, then to win one needs a majority of the votes cast:

> While we are always mindful of public relations techniques used commercially, we bear in mind the vast gulf between commercial public relations programs and political programs; namely, a commercial program may be a tremendous success in selling a 2 percent market. Our program is apt to be a failure unless it "sells" at least 50 percent of the voter market.[21]

This need to get enough votes to win is generally recognized as a prime motivating factor for democratic politicians. But votes aren't desirable *per se*. Votes are instrumentally useful to gain victory and its spoils. And in a democracy, votes are thought to be the link between the political leader and the group interests. Thus, for many, the ideal democratic politician may well be characterized as win-oriented, or even more specifically, a specialist in increasing his probability of gaining and holding office. This has been true of positive as well as normative theorists. Thus, a number of explanations of political behavior contain the premise that the politician is win-oriented. For example, Mayhew begins his work on Congress by revealing, "The discussion to come will hinge on the assumption that United States

---

[20]We do not deny that some differences in motives exists (indeed section IV of this chapter is devoted to one motivational type).

[21]Quoted in Stanley Kelley, Jr. *Professional Public Relations and Political Power*, Baltimore, Maryland: the John Hopkins Press, 1956, p. 46 fn.

congressmen are interested in getting re-elected—indeed, in their role here as abstractions, interested in nothing else."[22] Of course, if politicians are attempting to increase the expected value of their rewards, they would be concerned with winning only if they felt their personal actions could affect their probability of being in office.

This last caveat, that the politician must feel that he can affect the likelihood of staying in office, is of crucial importance. Again, Mayhew asks, "Even if congressmen are singlemindedly interested in re-election, are they in a position as individuals to do anything about it? If they are not, if they are inexorably shoved to and fro by forces in their political environments, then obviously it makes no sense to pay much attention to their individual activities."[23] But even if national political events, such as wars and prosperity, are major factors affecting the fortunes of congressmen (especially the fortunes of those who do not come from "safe districts"), they are still able to affect the percentages in their own primary and general elections . . . [or] they think they can" and "there is reason for them to try to do so."[24]

Anthony Downs' widely celebrated theory of democratic politics is built upon premises like these. He translates desire to win into a drive by parties and candidates to maximize their votes.[25] But given that it is costly to acquire additional votes, this translation is Downs' undoing. Why should a democratic entrepreneur be interested in securing any votes beyond the number necessary to win? One possible motive for attempting a larger majority (or plurality) is the uncertainty attendant upon electoral contests. Politicians rarely, if ever, have enough information about the way in which the vote is going to break, to cut short all vote seeking activity. But even though politicians always seem to hedge their bets by seeking additional votes as insurance, they still won't want to maximize votes.

> No doubt any congressman would engage in an act to raise his November figure from 80 percent to 90 percent if he could be absolutely sure that the act would accomplish the end (without affecting his primary percentage) and if it could be undertaken at low personal cost. But still, trying to "win comfortably" is not the same as trying to win all the popular vote. As the personal cost (e.g. expenditure of personal energy) of a hypothetical "sure gain" rises, the congressman at the 55 percent November level is more likely to be willing to pay it than his colleague at the 80 percent level."[26]

Historical evidence exists to illustrate the point: "safe congressmen" do less to improve their chances of victory incrementally. Indeed, the subjective feeling of safety can be the very key to the displacing of a well entrenched congressman. The case of Emanuel Celler, from Brooklyn, illustrates this well. As Jimmy Breslin described it,

[22]Mayhew, *op. cit.*, p. 13.
[23]*Ibid.*, pp. 17–18.
[24]*Ibid.*, p. 33.
[25]Anthony Downs, *An Economic Theory of Democracy*, New York: Harper and Row, 1957. In this work Downs assumes that there is only one office and that parties are unified teams of workers who try to get their candidate elected.
[26]Mayhew, *op. cit.*, pp. 46–47.

Meade [H. Esposito, the Democratic leader of Brooklyn] then held up a plaque.

"Here, see what they did for me? They gave me a plaque. That's Manny Celler's work. He has all the congressmen and senators give me a plaque for political leadership. Isn't that something?" . . .

"He gives me a plaque and I'm supposed to make sure everything is all right in his district. He never comes around. Well, what's the difference? I'll take care of things for him."

"He has no trouble, has he?"

"Well, there's some broad says she's going to run against him in the primary or something. You know these freaking broads. Who knows what she wants? It don't matter. How the hell can you run against the Chairman of the House Judiciary Committee? Manny's a national landmark."

On a morning a month later, I stopped into Woerner's Restaurant on Remsen Street in Brooklyn, just downstairs from Esposito's headquarters, and Meade, in a back booth, waved for me to sit down.

"I don't know what to do, I can't get this freakin' Liz Holtzman out of the race."

"Who is that?"

"The broad running against Manny Celler."

"Well, is it a fight, or what?"

"Nah. Shouldn't be a fight. It's just that this Manny, you know, he never comes around. And I hear this girl, she's got all kinds of young girls running around for her. Indians. Freaking squaws. I've tried to talk her out of the race, but it looks like I can't do it. Maybe Manny better get his ass up here and see some people. That plaque he gave me can't go out and campaign for him."

On March 29, Elizabeth Holtzman, a thirty-year-old attorney, announced she was running in the Democratic primary against Emanuel Celler, eighty-four, the famous Chairman of the House Judiciary Committee.

"As far as I'm concerned, she doesn't exist," Celler announced.

The years had destroyed Celler's ability to see. By this time he thought of himself as actually holding power, rather than holding the illusion of power.

The next morning, Ms. Holtzman was on the subway platform handing out literature describing Celler's interest in legislation that helped Fishback & Moore, a company he held interest in.

Only 23 percent of the people in the district voted in the June primary. Elizabeth Holtzman received 15,596 votes; Emanuel Celler had 14,896. By the margin of 610, she was in Congress.[27]

When support is costly, politicians are win-oriented rather than vote-maximizing.[28] Indeed, Downs' argument is jeopardized precisely by the rational calculus he proposed.

But Mayhew and Downs must face other problems. The expected value maximizer will normally be interested in more than the holding of office. Indeed, both Mayhew and Downs recognize that votes are only instrumen-

[27]Jimmy Breslin, *How the Good Guys Finally Won,* New York: Ballantine Books, 1976, pp. 87–89.

[28]For further analysis of this point, the reader should look at Joseph A. Schlesinger, "The Primary Goals of Political Parties: A Clarification of Positive Theory, *American Political Science Review,* LXIX, No. 3, Sept. 1975. pp. 840–849, and Mayhew, *op. cit.,* pp. 46–47.

tally useful for the politician in his search for rewards of office.[29] Under such circumstances, however, the win-orientation of the politician is less likely to be accurate. Indeed, even the plausibility of vote maximization may be enhanced when the rewards of office are considered. For the politician can increase his rewards by winning big.

To begin with, a massive victory can increase the security of a politician. And security can lead to a variety of substantial rewards. To the extent that an incumbent has demonstrated his ability to construct a large coalition of supporters, others thinking of opposing him in future elections will perceive a higher barrier to surmount. Again, as Mayhew points out:

> The logic here is that a narrow victory (in primary or general election) is a sign of weakness that can inspire hostile political actors to deploy resources intensively the next time around. By this reasoning, the higher the election percentages the better.[30]

Since some potential opponents may be scared off by massive victories, the incumbent may avoid costly renomination or re-election fights. Thus, there are cost-saving reasons for expanding one's votes beyond the bare minimum. But this concern with long-term cost saving isn't the same as vote maximizing. After all, what the politician thinks he can save in the future will determine what he is willing to spend to get votes today.

A large electoral victory can do more than save costs. It can also increase the stream of positive rewards available to a winner. When a politician has a large electoral base, people are likely to expect him to retain his office over time. Consequently they will expect him to be in a position of political influence in the future. To the extent that the ability to deliver political favors increases with increasing seniority, the anticipation of seniority may be a decided asset. Individuals who anticipate the need for long-run favors from government like to make deals with politicians who will continue to be in office.

Thus, taken together, there are various positive benefits that can accrue to the politician who seeks a larger than minimum electoral coalition. Given these incentives, democratic politicians holding well rewarded offices often will be interested in increasing their share of the vote beyond that amount barely necessary to win. But the vote-maximizing hypothesis is tenable only if there is a continuing net incentive to get more votes. That is, the expected marginal return from *each* additional vote must be greater than the marginal cost of that vote. This condition is not very likely to hold in many situations.

Thus, neither of the ideal forms of democratic politician are likely to be found in the real world. We would not expect to find vote *maximizers,* although many politicians may attempt to get many votes beyond the bare minimum. And we would not expect to find politicians who are exclusively interested in winning, or electoral victory, because the rewards and costs of office are not absolutely fixed. Actions taken by competitors and incumbents

[29]Downs, *op. cit.,* pp. 30–31.
[30]Mayhew, *op. cit.,* p. 46.

can affect what they get. And if we assume that rational individuals are concerned with maximizing expected value, it follows that politicians will allocate some of their effort and resources to the problem of increasing their rewards rather than just worrying about holding on to office. Examples of how politicians can profit (both legally and illegally) from manipulation of programs are legion. For the sake of a simple empirical referent, however, consider the following way in which George Wallace chose to increase his personal revenue at the expense of his campaign coffers, and therefore at some marginal cost to his election chances.

> Gov. George C. Wallace of Alabama is paying himself personal "royalties" from his Presidential campaign treasury for the use of his own likeness in political materials.
>
> The Wallace campaign's financial reports to the Federal monitoring authorities indicate that the Governor got $14,999 in royalties in two payments last year.
>
> According to Wallace headquarters in Montgomery, most of the 1974 total was paid for an impression of Mr. Wallace's face on silver medallions coined at the Franklin Mint, a commercial operation, and offered in a campaign mailing to contributors of $25 or more.
>
> Mr. Wallace's conversion of political funds to private income, openly reported but heretofore unnoticed, is viewed as legally safe but politically risky.[31]

One could catalog almost indefinitely opportunities inherent in democratic political offices for manipulation of rewards to incumbents. And opportunities for increasing self-gratification are not limited to democratic political entrepreneurs. Tribal chiefs, oriental despots, and medieval lords, all seem to demonstrate a substantial concern with the rewards attendant upon their offices and undertake activities to increase their returns.[32] In all such cases, we would expect the rational entrepreneur to invest in both increasing returns and increasing security to increase his total expected returns.

We can get a sense of the pattern of these investments from a discussion of politics in a more despotic vein. Consider the description of feudal politics by Thompson and Johnson. They carefully lay out the details of the investment pattern of feudal lords to raise resources and to keep their positions (as well as their lives). Thompson and Johnson focus on the supply of selective incentives for the raising of resources for community projects and personal enrichment. Positive incentives were possible because the lord had the ability to monopolize the sale of desired goods. Negative incentives were maintained by relatively large, and visible, coercive forces that were used both to extract taxes and to protect the lord from ambitious rivals or serfs.

[31]New York Times, May 16, 1975, p. 9.
[32]Examples of activities of each entrepreneur can be found respectively in I. Schapera, *Government and Politics in Tribal Societies*, New York: Schocken, 1967; Karl Wittvogel, *Oriental Despotism*, New Haven: Yale University Press, 1957; and James W. Thompson and Edgar N. Johnson, *An Introduction to Medieval Europe 300–1500*, New York: W. W. Norton, 1937; and Fredrik Barth, *Political Leadership Among Swat Pathans*, New York: Humanities Press, 1965.

A variety of taxes were levied upon the serfs. To insure that these taxes were paid, the entrepreneur had to have sufficient coercion to make it "worthwhile" for the serf to pay the taxes. But the entrepreneur's investment in coercion brought other returns. Coercion was used to establish, and protect, the monopolistic sale of private goods. Indeed, coercion could be used to insure a market for these goods even when the serfs preferred not to purchase any. Thus, when conditions changed, and an erstwhile valued good lost some of its glitter, serfs could be forced to use the goods and services to insure revenue flows to the lords. Often the serf was in the position of involuntary customer:

> . . . [S]pecial fees were collected for the use of those kinds of manorial land that were not divided up among the tenant peasantry, such as pasture, woodland, and waste land.

> Akin to these were the fees collected by the lord for the use of certain of his properties on the manor. Since the peasant was obliged to use them whether he would or no, they were in effect monopolies, although in origin they may have been only the means of providing for the peasant what he could not provide for himself. These fees were called banalities. The lord owned the mill, the bake-oven, the wine press, the brewhouse, sometimes even the village well and the village bull. Often these monopolies were not administered directly by his agents but were farmed out for rent. Every serf on the manor was required to bring his grain to the lord's mill, his flour to the lord's oven, his grapes to the lord's wine press, his barley to the lord's brewhouse, his cows to the lord's bull, and for each of these services there was a fee. The records of the manorial courts are full of attempts of the peasants to avoid these monopolies, especially when, as in the case of grinding grain or baking bread, the work could easily be done at home . . . Finally, the lord often enjoyed a monopoly of the sale of wine in the village for a fixed period at definite times of the year, and the peasant was required to take a certain amount whether he wanted to or not. Instances are recorded where, "if a man refused to take the prescribed quantity of wine, it was poured into his cottage under the threshold or through the hen-hole; or it was put into a pig-trough." And on a German manor, "if the tenant have not drunk his . . . two gallons, . . ., then the lord shall pour a four-gallon measure over the man's roof; if the wine runs down the tenant must pay for it; if it runs upwards he shall pay nothing."[33]

In principle the medieval entrepreneur could tax and assess fees at his own discretion. But consideration for his security set limitations upon the returns he could expect from his investment. As Thompson and Johnson note:

> Besides, every sensible lord realized that to have a contented peasantry it was neither prudent nor safe to resort to arbitrary exactions. Moreover, the Church was careful to warn the nobility. "The great must make themselves loved by the small. They must be careful not to inspire hate. The humble must not be scorned; if they can aid us, they can also do us harm. You know that many serfs have killed their masters or have burnt their houses."[34]

[33]Thompson and Johnson, *op. cit.*, pp. 332–333, as quoted from G. G. Coulton, *The Medieval Village*, Cambridge: Ouly Press, 1925, p. 60.
[34]Thompson and Johnson, *op. cit.*, p. 331.

Clearly entrepreneurs of the time were concerned in distributing their investments over their two basic concerns in an efficient fashion. In general, that is what is to be expected of the rational entrepreneurial politician, in a democratic, or feudal, context.

We began by noting that democratic politicians are, ideally, interested only in winning or votes. Even though the ideal may not have empirical versimilitude, it does serve as a heuristic device for thinking about the incentive systems faced by real political leaders in democratic, and other, contexts. In all these cases, the entrepreneurs face explicit threats of replacement. This concern is a major determinant of their investment strategies. In a parallel fashion, it is helpful to discuss the ideal that is the polar opposite of the ideal democrat: the leader who can concentrate entirely on maximizing the returns from his office and who spends nothing on securing his tenure.

Bureaucratic Contexts

What is the identifying characteristic of a context in which an entrepreneur will not invest to secure his tenure?[35] Theoretically, the conditions under which an entrepreneur would be rational to specialize in this way are that his tenure be fixed or that he cannot change his probability of holding office.

Although political entrepreneurs rarely will be able to do *nothing* to affect their probability of holding office, some political contexts may approach or approximate that condition quite closely. For example, the head of a large bureaucracy may enjoy a tenure that he is relatively unable to manipulate.[36] If so, he need not concern himself with investing his resources on increments in his probability of holding office. Thus, the rational leader will concentrate on increasing the reward stream that he enjoys from his position.

Indeed, William Niskanen argues that the behavior of leaders of bureaucracies can be understood as the result of a bureaucrat-entrepreneur's attempts to increase the bureau's budget.[37] From this assumption, Niskanen predicts the behavior of bureaus, as well as bureaucrats.[38] But since the reward stream of the bureaucrat needn't be directly related to the size of the bureau's budget, recent formulations of these models have been altered. Current formulations are developed on the assumption that the bureau-

---

[35]For a more formal analysis, see Frohlich and Oppenheimer, "The Carrot and the Stick: Optimal Program Mixes for Entrepreneurial Political Leaders." *Public Choice*, XIX, Fall 1974, pp. 43–61.

[36]In the U.S. judges are also often in this situation.

[37]William Niskanen, *Bureaucracy and Representative Government*. Chicago: Aldine, 1971. Precursors of his analysis which use a rationality perspective but do not formalize their results are Anthony Downs, *Inside Bureaucracy*, Boston: Little Brown, 1967 and Gordon Tullock, *The Politics of Bureaucracy*. Washington D.C.: Public Affairs Press, 1965.

[38]For example, Niskanen has developed conditions under which the output of the bureau will be suboptimal, as well as inefficient. Applications of this model have been used to analyze the relative strengths and weaknesses of various structural alternatives to government, including "multifunctional," general purpose governments to "special district" governments such as port authorities, sewer districts, school boards, etc. See Richard E. Wagner and Warren E. Weber, "Competition Monopoly, and the Organization of Government in Metropolitan Areas," *National Bureau of Economic Research*, New York: April, 1975, mimeo.

cratic leaders are concerned with increasing their discretionary budget, i.e. the revenue that they can receive above and beyond that needed to perform the functions absolutely required of them by their mission description.[39]

Although the Niskanen model is helpful in illuminating a variety of bureau activities, Julius Margolis has criticized it for its failure to take into account that many high level bureaucrats work in an environment of multiple offices affording the opportunity for both horizontal and vertical job mobility.[40] To the extent that differential rewards accompany such moves, bureaucrats will be concerned with investments to obtain those rewards. Thus, if their actions can lead to greater opportunities, they will become concerned with tenure and mobility questions, as were the politicians we examined in the previous sections. That is, manipulable possibilities of demotion and promotion (either lateral or vertical) will substantially modify their incentives. Much as we modified the ideal democrats' incentive from a purely win-motivated orientation, we would modify the ideal bureaucrats' incentives from a purely reward-stream orientation. For bureaucrats, the change in motivation follows from the multiple office context, and a similar introduction of multiple offices into our analysis of electoral political contexts would now be in order.

Multiple-Office Contexts

Most political contexts involve many political offices, many political leaders, and many competitors. Some attempts have recently been made to develop multi-office models. For example, Gordon Black's work on multiple-office electoral politics is developed on an assumed hierarchy of political offices.[41] The hierarchy forms a career ladder with transferable investment costs. Black assumes that the investment made to obtain one office can be used to get another (higher) office, but it cannot be similarly used for nonpolitical advancement. Since, as he notes, higher offices are more costly than lower ones, additional investments are needed to obtain them. However, higher offices also offer greater rewards:

> . . . as the costs of an office increase, the benefits to be gained from that office must increase faster than costs, such that the net benefit from the more costly position is greater than the net benefit from the less costly position. If this were

[39]A discussion of this modification of Niskanen's original thesis that bureaucrats attempt to maximize their budgets is given by Jean-Luc Migúex and Gerard Bélangér in "Toward a General Theory of Managerial Discretion," *Public Choice*, 17, Spring 1974, pp. 27–43 and in the exchange with Niskanen that follows. Also see William Niskanen, "Bureaucracy and the Interests of Bureaucrats," paper delivered at Conference on the Economic Analysis of Political Behavior, April 11–12, 1975, Cambridge, Mass.

[40]Margolis' critique was orally presented at the conference mentioned in footnote 39. But for a discussion of the effects of multiple offices on the career patterns of bureaucrats, see Eugene B. McGregor, Jr., "Politics and the Career Mobility of Bureaucrats," American Political Science Review, LXVIII, No. 1, March 1974, pp. 18–26.

[41]Gordon S. Black, "A Theory of Political Ambition: Career Choices and the Role of Structural Incentives," *American Political Science Review*, 66, No. 1, March 1972, pp. 144–159. Also see his "A Theory of Professionalization in Politics," *American Political Science Review*, **64**, No. 3, Sept. 1970. pp. 865–78.

not the case, rational men would not seek to advance to more costly positions.[42]

In this situation, transferability of investment tends to lock individuals into political career sequences once they take the first few steps.

> ... as the individual increases his investment in the career sequence, the value of the next step upward or the next goal will also increase relative to alternatives outside the career sequence. In a sense, the individual's investments tend to pull him further and further into the sequence even though he may not have originally intended to follow the route on which he now finds himself.[43]

In other words, the competitors for higher offices will usually be political leaders from lower offices: a theoretical result certainly in conformity with most casual observations of politics.

Of course, the explicit introduction of multiple offices allows for the discussion of the interdependence of these offices. Black's argument indicates a certain type of interdependence: one of hierarchical recruitment patterns and career patterns. But with multiple offices other interdependencies are possible. For example, Mayhew considers a legislature a context with a relative equality of offices. All legislators are engaged in the producing of a "common output." In this sense, their legislative product is a collective good for all legislators. If the members don't campaign as members of a party, but rather as individual members of the legislature, they are faced with a dilemma: what can they do to get support? It is difficult for any *one* of them to use the legislative output as a means for gaining support in his individualistic fight for survival as a legislator. For we have here an application of the theory developed in Chaps. 3 and 4 regarding collective goods. What is needed is a system of selective incentives to get the congressional members to contribute to the business of Congress.

> [C]redit (or blame) would attach ... to the doings of the government as a whole. But there are 535 [members]. Hence it becomes necessary for each congressman to try to peel off pieces of governmental accomplishment for which he can believably generate a sense of responsibility ... [t]he staple way of doing this is to traffic in what may be called "particularized benefits."[44]

There needs to be mutually beneficial trades and favors between office holders to enable each congressman to peel off pieces of governmental accomplishment.

Indeed, whenever there are numerous office holders, they are likely to have common interests. Such common interests could involve the financing of campaigns, the running of elections in a manner that excludes certain competitors, the agreement to work for certain kinds of policies, etc. Such interests can serve as the basis for a political party or political machine. An

---

[42]*Ibid.*, p. 154.
[43]*Ibid.*, p. 156.
[44]Mayhew, *op. cit.*, p. 53. Mayhew has a discussion of these particularized benefits.

entrepreneur could invest to set up an organization to supply collective goods to office holders.

What activity could such an entrepreneur undertake? He could engineer sets of beneficial trades. For example, where candidates for office fail to get elected, he may find them appointed jobs through other, more fortunate candidates. Those who help elect officers would be similarly rewarded. The "Boss" might even enter into deals with potential competitors to buy them off and make more secure the life of a variety of his minions over time. Sayre and Kaufman in discussing politics in New York give examples of the widespread use of appointive power to reward party supporters by giving them positions in the court system.[45] And Plunkitt points out how security for workers is maintained over time by reciprocity in patronage between parties.

> Let me tell you, too, that I got jobs from Republicans in office—Federal and otherwise. When Tammany's on top I do good turns for the Republicans. When they're on top they don't forget me.

> Me and the Republicans are enemies just one day in the year—election day. Then we fight tooth and nail. The rest of the time it's live and let live with us.[46]

Such investment of costly and valuable patronage jobs in the present to protect against possible future losses (political insurance so to speak) is but one form of activity undertaken to preserve the viability of the machine over time. All of these aspects of his job creates considerable organizational needs for the machine politician.

James Q. Wilson discusses in detail the competing demands on the entrepreneur in charge of a political machine.[47] Wilson emphasizes that the party boss's job is to maintain both the machine over time, and (of course) his position as head of the organization. This concern will decrease the orientation of the party's candidates toward winning, or getting votes, in each *particular* electoral contest. The maintainence of the party machinery and the defense of the party bureaucrats will be of concern in choosing the candidates who run, the issues they (are allowed to, or encouraged to) raise, and the types of campaign tactics they employ. Although the party machine may be made up of office holders, this need not be the case, and in any event, the machine contains a set of offices that parallel the public offices to be co-ordinated. Daley, for example, may have been the mayor of Chicago, but he was also the head of the county Democratic organization. And the two offices are separable. In fact, Daley did have two offices, even if they were only separated by a door. He held two posts, but the reward structures and security of tenure in each were intricately interwoven with one another and with those of other offices.

[45]Wallace S. Sayre and Herbert Kaufman, *Governing New York City,* New York: Norton, 1965, Chap. 14.
[46]*Ibid,* p. 38.
[47]James Q. Wilson, "The Economy of Patronage," *American Political Science Review,* **69,** Aug. 1961, pp. 369–380.

Conclusions

The more general point, by now, must be clear. The role of political leader, as specified in the first and second section of this chapter, is underspecified. Details of the political context within which the leader is operating must be filled in before one can explain or predict the behavior of a rational entrepreneur even if one knows the values of the individual involved. The context structures the incentives that the individual responds to and, as such, determines the behavior he or she will choose. Moreover, the theory of collective goods specifies variables which are important in the differentiation of political contexts. The size and types of rewards available to political leaders play a crucial role in determining behavior. These must be spelled out in making any preliminary comparisons. Secondly, we are forced to examine the structure of competition for the occupancy of the leadership roles. One aspect of this question is the expected fate of political leaders who use vast proportions of the resources for self-aggrandizement rather than for the collective goods. Another is the likely role to be played by a defeated politician. Is it citizen in exile, or prisoner to be executed, or retired professional to be venerated? Furthermore, the theory points to the politician's ability to affect his rewards and his probability of staying in office. Finally, the structure of the multiple offices in the political system is of crucial importance in the examination for broader political machines and alliances. Controlling for these variables, we should be able to develop theoretical predictions of a considerable portion of leadership behavior.

III. NON SELF-ORIENTED ENTREPRENEURS: WHAT DIFFERENCE?

So far the discussion of entrepreneurial behavior has been based upon on the assumption that entrepreneurs are self-interested. We could certainly protest that this is too narrow a view of entrepreneurial motivation. Some leaders appear not to be motivated by the material rewards available from successful organizing. Some successful political leaders remain poor to their dying days, apparently interested only in the welfare of the group. Although this kind of "altruistic" leader does occasionally make an appearance on the political stage, it is our conjecture that (1) altruistic politicians are likely to be no more frequent than "dedicated" doctors, or benevolent businessmen; and yet, (2) altruistic leadership may play a crucial role in the quality of political outcomes. This is so even though (3) altruistic and self-interested leaders are likely to behave similarly in a wide variety of contexts.

Consider our first conjecture. What reasons are there to believe that one is no more likely to encounter an altruistic politician than an altruistic lawyer (or whatever). Suppose a group is fortunate enough to have had an altruistic and successful leader. Presumably that leader labored to organize the group and to provide it with a variety of collective benefits that would increase the welfare of the population and satisfy their most crying needs. Under those circumstances, there is a drop in the potential rewards for altruistic leadership in the next "generation" of leadership. Altruism may be sufficient inducement when needs cry out to be met, but as Michels has written:

> For the great majority of men, idealism alone is an inadequate incentive for the fulfillment of duty. Enthusiasm is not an article which can be kept long in store. Men who will stake their bodies and their lives for a moment, or even for some months in succession, on behalf of a great idea often prove incapable of permanent work in the service of the same idea even when the sacrifices demanded are comparatively trifling. The joy of self-sacrifice is comparable to a fine gold coin which can be spent grandly all at once, whereas if we change it into small coin it dribbles imperceptibly away. Consequently, . . ., it is necessary that the leaders should receive a prosaic reward in addition to the devotion of their comrades and the satisfaction of a good conscience.[48]

The very success of an altruistic leader makes further altruistic actions by others (or the same leader) less attractive.[49]

If an altruistic leader is involved in the original organizing of a group, he will either uncover the possibility of generating material rewards in the process, or he won't. If the group is never able to properly reward potential leaders, the job performed by the altruistic leader will have been (in all likelihood) irreplaceable. Once he is gone, the distinct possibility exists that the group will be left without a "political" future. On the other hand, the organizing may uncover a means of tapping sufficient resources from the group so that the leadership position is attractive for others (i.e. nonaltruists). Indeed, for this to be the case, it need not be possible to repay the original organizing effort. For even if the organizing effort of the groups' founders cannot be repaid, it could still be possible to reward future leaders for the maintainance of the organization. Thus, it may take altruists to organize groups with limited resources, but self-interested and ambitious individuals could find a profitable career in running those organizations. An assymetry of motivations between generations of political leaders is most likely to come about whenever there are abnormally high "start-up costs" to the establishment of a group's political organization. So, it may take a John L. Lewis, or a Cesar Chavez to set up a union under conditions of terrible exploitation, but a Tony Boyle can take it over and run it once it has been organized.[50]

Both of these last points lead us to our second conjecture. For we can conclude that if there are high start up costs and relative deprivation of the group being organized, altruists will be overly represented in the class of "founding fathers" of organizations. When we consider other positions, those in the previously established political organizations, there is reason to argue that there will be an underrepresentation of altruistic leaders, especially when compared to the representation of altruists as doctors, etc. For

[48]Robert Michels, *Political Parties,* New York: Dover, 1959, p. 126.

[49]This observation was also made by Anthony Downs, *Inside Bureaucracy,* New York: Harper and Row, 1967. Especially see Chap. 8.

[50]Anthony Boyle was convicted, in 1974, for the slaying of Jock Yablonski, a political opponent who tried to run for the Presidency of the United Mine Workers. It was also charged that Boyle was involved in the fixing of elections, the diverting of union funds for personal use, and of entering into corrupt agreements with mine owners to the detriment of the miners.

"service jobs" in general are supplying excludable and divisible goods, and thus, each service worker (e.g. each doctor) is not likely to be "displaced" by competition. In the case of the political leader, however, displacement is the major way in which competitors relate. Thus, if nonaltruists are both numerous and good competitors (and why shouldn't they be?), they can be expected to gradually drive out the altruists rather than merely take over some of their "market share."

To conclude, it may well be that altruists perform politically irreplaceable functions as innovators and leaders of the relatively deprived. Yet it is likely that when successful, they are driven from their positions. In the economic realm their activity may be no more important, yet their tenure may be greater.

If politics is likely to discriminate against altruists, and altruists perform indispensible political functions, there still may be little difference in the behavior of altruists and self-interested politicians in many contexts.

Regardless of the motivations of a political leader, he must engage in exchanges or trades with other individuals to get things done. Therefore, he must pander to the interests, values, and needs of others. If he is to be successful in making these trades the leader must be a good student of human nature and motivations. Thus, even if the politician is a saint, he must be a salesman if he is to succeed. If one wants others to do something for you, one has to appeal to them on the basis of *their* self-interest. Given human nature, the appeals of the politician, must resemble the appeals of the salesman. One extremely successful organizer who appears to have been altruistically motivated saw this quite clearly and acted accordingly:

> In a mass organization you can't go outside of people's actual experience. I've been asked, for example, why I never talk to a Catholic priest or a Protestant minister or a rabbi in terms of the Judeo-Christian ethic or the Ten Commandments or the Sermon on the Mount. I never talk in these terms. Instead, I approach them on the basis of their own self-interest. . . .
>
> If I approached them in a moralistic way, it would be outside of their experience, because Christianity and Judeo-Christianity are outside of the experience of organized religion. They would just listen to me and very sympathetically tell me how noble I was. And the moment I walked out they'd call their secretaries in and say, "If that screw-ball ever shows up again, tell him I'm out."[51]

Thus, if the mass of humanity is basically self-interested, the leader (regardless of his or her *personal* motivation) will have to appeal to and mobilize this self-interest.

Notice that economists and other spectators of the human scene have long held self-interest as central in individual choices of occupations and in activities undertaken therein. Two hundred years ago Adam Smith wrote:

[51]Saul Alinsky as quoted in Marion K. Sanders, "The Professional Radical, *Harper's Magazine,* June 1965. Reported also in the introduction of Alinsky's *Reveille for Radicals,* Vintage Books edition, New York: Random House, 1969, p. xvi.

... [M]an has almost constant occasion for the help of his brethren, and it is in vain for him to expect it from their benevolence only. He will be more likely to prevail if he can interest their self-love in his favour, and shew them that it is; for their own advantage to do for him what he requires of them. Whoever offers to another a bargain of any kind, proposes to do this. Give me that which I want, and you shall have this which you want, is the meaning of every such offer; and it is in this manner that we obtain from one another the far greater part of those good offices which we stand in need of. It is not from the benevolence of the butcher, the brewer, or the baker, that we expect our dinner, but from their regard to their own self-interest. We address ourselves not to their humanity but to their self-love, and never talk to them of our own necessities but of their advantages.[52]

But these similarities should not obscure the real differences in which can be expected in the behavior of self-oriented and group-oriented leaders. Self-oriented leaders will demand and take a share of the collections for themselves. Group-oriented leaders will tend to ignore this basis for self-enrichment. When the extractive machinery of the political leader includes force and hence taxation, the potential for self-enrichment through coercion can be enormous. And in such coercive situations the differences, in terms of group welfare, between a self-interested and an altruistic (or non-materialisticly motivated) leader can be huge. Compare the benefits accruing to the Dominicans when the Dominican Republic was run by Trujillo and to the Chinese under Mao. Trujillo, by the time of his assassination, had amassed a personal fortune that included more than 75 percent of the total productive resources of his nation.[53] Had the proceeds of these resources been applied to social projects, obviously other members of the society would have benefited. Apparently, no such surplus was withheld from the Chinese by Mao.[54]

IV. THE ETHICS OF LEADERSHIP

Perhaps it was Machiavelli who first underscored the difficulty of reconciling Christian ethics and effective political leadership techniques.[55] If there was a conflict between political and personal (or public and private) ethics, Machiavelli supported the political. Machiavelli set effective, collective effort as a logical precondition for the establishment and maintenance of a society that would allow individuals to live a moral private life. The theory devel-

---

[52]Adam Smith, *The Wealth of Nations*, New York: Modern Library, 1937, p. 14.

[53]Trujillo was perhaps the self-interested despot *extrordinaire*. Robert D. Crassweller's *Trujillo*, New York: Macmillan, 1966 is an eye opening political biography.

[54]This does not mean to say that second generational leadership will not skim a higher percentage from the Chinese. Compare, for example, the original government in the Soviet Union after the revolution with the crass excesses of the Stalin era. See Aleksandr Isayevich Solzhenitsyn, *The Gulag Archipelago, 1918–1956*, New York: Harper and Row, 1973.

[55]Isiah Berlin, "The Question of Machiavelli," *New York Review of Books*, XVII, No. 7, Nov. 4, 1971, pp. 20–32, and the exchange in the same journal, April 6, 1972, pp. 35–37, analyzes Machiavelli from this perspective.

oped in the previous chapters supports Machiavelli on both points. Personal and political ethics are likely to conflict. If personal ethics has to do with such things as charity, improving the lot of the unfortunate, etc., then personal ethics will require effective political action. Hence any system of personal ethics that precludes effective political action may be seen to be contradictory.[56]

Certainly, personal ethics and political efficacy are likely to conflict. Effective organizers must often set up incentives independent from the collective goods to which the group aspires. Leaders usually cannot appeal to the higher interests of the individuals to enable the group to achieve its goals. Furthermore, the leader must be capable of protecting his resource stream, which is likely to be based on positive and negative "private good" rewards. The protection of the resource stream usually involves the establishment of a monopoly (as in examples above from the middle ages) and/or a coercive organization for taxation. Both situations lead to morally reprehensible interactions with others. Both situations require the same sort of guile and willingness to coerce as Machiavelli discussed with reference to the role of princes. But these situations are not restricted to princes: they have a general applicability to group politics of all types: labor unions, business associations, charities, and lobby groups.

Even the displacement of altruistic leaders raises serious ethical questions regarding what ethical altruists should do. If politicians are threatened with displacement (rather than the mere loss of a percentage of clients) what instrumentalities are justified in their attempts to hold on to their offices?

> There are even occasional congressmen who intentionally do things that make their own electoral survival difficult or impossible . . ., Former Senator Paul Douglas (D., Ill.) tells of how he tried to persuade Senator Frank Graham (D., N.C.) to tailor his issue positions in order to survive a 1950 primary. Graham, a liberal appointee to the office, refused to listen. He was a "saint," says Douglas. He lost his primary. There are not many saints.[57]

But do not altruists have an ethical obligation to try to stay in office? Indeed are the morally necessary leaders justified in *not* fighting hard to stay in office?[58] Of course, the questions are not easy to answer, but they are definitely raised by both the divorcing of the incentives from the collective good and the structure of political competitions. And they lead directly to the difficulties in answering the question: "How can we judge political actions?" And here there are no easy answers. Perhaps one is thrown back

[56]The latter point stems from the fact that the distribution of income has its public good aspects. See L. C. Thurow, "The Income Distribution as a Pure Public Good," *Quarterly Journal of Economics*, Vol 85, No. 2, 1971, on this point. Furthermore, since there may be other ethical considerations than economic deprivation, the general observation that the attainment of a common interest involves a collective good (Olson, *op. cit.,*) is of importance here.

[57]Mayhew op. cit., pp. 15–16, who cites Paul H. Douglas, *In the Fullness of Time*, New York: Harcourt Brace Jovanovich, 1972, pp. 238–241.

[58]For e.g., was Ralph, in William Golding's *Lord of the Flies*, justified in not taking violent steps to prevent the take-over by Jack? Could his defense be made in terms of "law and order" or were the even more fundamental issues at stake, including the prevention of slavery torture, murder, etc.?

to the question of does the end justify the means, or, if the end does *not* justify the means, what does?

V. FOR FURTHER READING

Aside from those pieces obviously emphasized in the footnotes, two other items usefully could be read for an introduction to the analysis of leadership. Gerald Kraemer, in his "A Dynamical Model of Political Equilibrium," *Cowles Discussion Paper* No. 396, New Haven: Yale 1975 proves a number of interesting theorems regarding the interactions (in a democracy) of vote-maximizing politicians. Donald Wittman, in his papers "Equilibrium Strategies By Policy Maximizing Candidates" and "Policy Maximizing Candidates: A Dynamical Model," *Journal of Economic Theory* (forthcoming) develops a generalized psychological model of the politician: that of a "policy preference maximizer." That is, Wittman considers the politician as having stakes in the outcomes, without specifying their characteristics. He than asks how do the politicians' preferences over outcomes effect their choice of strategy. These alternative formulations of the psyche of the politician are useful to contrast in attempting to develop any general formulation of the political process.

THE POLITICAL ECONOMY OF DEMOCRACY

"... There are some arts whose products are not judged solely, or best, by the artists themselves, namely, those arts whose products are recognized even by those who do not possess the art; for example, the knowledge of the house is not limited to the builder only; the user, or, in other words, the master, of the house will even be a better judge than the builder ... and the guest will judge better of a feast than the cook."[1] It is with this sort of perspective that the first great defense of democracy was written. Aristotle felt that the individuals ruled by a government might best be in a position to determine the value of that government. From that time to the present, the notion of democracy has been posited on citizen evaluation and determination of governmental programs. And since there are many citizens in any democracy, a democratic system requires that a multitude of judgments be aggregated into a single decision. The problem of how individuals are to be counted and weighed against one another is central to such a process. In "direct democracies," such as we often imagine existed in town meetings in colonial America, citizens are each asked to judge in every collective decision.[2] Many committees and legislatures may still operate in approximately this fashion.

On the other hand, in larger groups, direct democracy is likely to prove impossible. As Michels wrote in 1915:

> The sovereign masses are altogether incapable of undertaking the most necessary resolutions. The impotence of direct democracy, like the power of indirect democracy, is a direct outcome of the influence of number. In a polemic against Proudhon (1849), Louis Blanc asks whether it is possible for thirty-four millions of human beings (the population of France at that time) to carry on

[1]Aristotle, *Politics*, Book III, Chap. 11, p. 1191–2, *The Basic Works of Aristotle*, New York: Random House, 1941. (B. Jowett translation as revised by W. D. Ross.)
[2]But see Robert Dahl, *Who Governs?*, New Haven: Yale University Press, 1961, Chap. 2 for a different perspective on these meetings.

their affairs without accepting what the pettiest man of business finds necessary, the intermediation of representatives. He answers his own question by saying that one who declares direct action on this scale to be possible is a fool, and that one who denies its possibility need not be an absolute opponent of the idea of the state.[3]

Of course, the term democracy has been extended to cover what we often refer to as *representative democratic systems*. In such systems citizens freely select (i.e. judge) representatives who then collectively determine governmental policy. Yet in representative democracies, as in direct democracies, individual judgements are combined to reach collective decisions. The voting system by which these judgements are combined is a central element of the democratic arrangements.

Given any democratic system, we will want to know what differences an individual can make on the group choice and how he can make them. When there is a representative system, this problem translates into the relationship between the desires of the citizens and the policies of the government. As phrased, the subject is vast, indeed, too vast for current purposes. However, we shall attempt, in the next chapters, to identify characteristics of the relationship between actions by citizens and group choice in democracies. We will begin, in Chap. 5, by examining the act of voting by a rational individual in a representative democracy. What determines whether an individual will vote or not? Who will an individual vote for? These, and other characteristics of voting, may be interesting in themselves, but they also are major building blocks to reach further conclusions regarding the relationships between ruled and rulers in democracies. But before analyzing voting *per se,* let us more carefully consider the formal characteristics of democracy.

I. DEMOCRACY AS A SET OF DECISIONS RULES

Certainly, there are almost as many definitions of democracy as there are democratic political theorists. Central to most definitions, however, is the notion of a set of rules determining how certain group decisions will be made. At a more general level, democracies entail some set of *decision rules* for reaching specified types of group decisions.

In general, a set of decision rules specifies:

1. a category of group choices to be decided by employing the rules;
2. a set of resources (and their distribution among members of the group, if necessary) to be used in reaching the group decision;
3. how, when used, the resources are to be aggregated to yield a group choice.

Decision rules need not be democratic. Thus, a decision rule may include an agreement to be governed by a dictatorial monarch. Such an agreement would *ipso facto* specify certain geneological characteristics of

[3]Robert Michels, *Political Parties,* New York: The Free Press, 1962, p. 65.

individuals as crucial resources in the "weighing of individuals" for the reaching of group decisions. For example, in questions of succession, the seniority of living offspring might be the crucial decision variable. Implicitly, any decision rule excludes the use of other procedures for reaching group choices in the specified categories of decisions. Note, however, that there is nothing guaranteed about this prohibition. Violations of any decision rule are the stuff of coups, revolutions, and constitutional crises.

Of course, when the decision rule is not followed, the costs of political participation can rise rapidly. Consider what happens when the agreement underlying a democratic rule breaks down. Describing the act of voting in the Southern United States at the time of the Populist Movement, V. O. Key reported:

> To maintain an opposition party based on the dispossessed is a difficult political feat; it can be kept alive only if it has enough men of economic independence and substance to provide a continuing leadership. The story is not well documented, yet it is apparent from scattered evidence that the Bourbon Democrats, to liquidate the opposition, must have applied with savagery all the social and economic sanctions available. The "better," the "respectable" classes were threatened, and no fastidious regard for legality or morality checked the use of any measure that would contribute to their defense. "There is record," says Woodward, "of Populists' being turned out of church, driven from their homes, and refused credit because of their beliefs . . . A Southern Populist leader told a Western writer, 'The feeling of the Democracy against us is one of murderous hate. I have been shot at many times, Grand juries will not indict our assailants. Courts give us no protection.' " Not only were Populist leaders subjected to these pressures. In Augusta, Georgia, for example, the " 'Job-lash' was used . . . to force mill employees, white and black, to vote 'regular.' Some who refused to heed the warning were discharged." All the techniques of private economic coercion and intimidation came into play to weaken the rebel ranks—armies that are by their nature poorly disciplined.[4]

Similarly, the violence associated with the attempt to register blacks as voters in the South during the civil rights movement in the 1960's can be seen as the acts associated with rejection, by some individuals, of the group's "official" decision rule: one man, one vote.

Since a decision rule specifies that a particular set of resources "counts" in political contexts, these resources gain value from the additional uses to which they can be put under the rule. Thus, votes, created by a democracy for nonmarket use, can eventually develop a market value. Payments by lobbyists for legislators' votes as well as similar deals by machine politicians for the votes of the average citizen are a consequence of the specification of votes as the resource to be used in reaching group decisions.

But democracy is a decision rule with special characteristics. For our purposes it will be useful to identify the characteristics that distinguish democratic rules from all other sorts of rules. To do so, we shall lean heavily

[4]V. O. Key, Jr., *Southern Politics in State and Nation,* New York: Knopf, 1949. p. 553.

on the formulations of Robin Farquharson.[5] His analysis requires the use
of three basic terms, which he described as follows:

> First, voters. We assume that there exist a number of individuals, whose
> choices have consequences. These voters may compose an electorate, an as-
> sembly, or a committee: they may even be viewed as blocs or parties, or nations
> in conclave. The only essential assumption is that they constitute units, each
> with the power to choose, and that the choices made by all the individuals
> determine a result. This result will necessarily be a member of the set of
> outcomes.
>
> The outcomes are the possible results of the process of decision. The voting
> must eventually terminate with the selection of one or other outcome. . . .
>
> With regard to the outcomes, each voter has preferences.[6]

Preferences and outcomes we have dealt with before, of course. Voters are
the new element. Discussing voters who face a choice between two outcomes, Farquharson says:

> He may choose either one or the other. The choices expressed by all the
> voters determine the subset which is selected. Such a process may reasonably
> be called "voting" only if the relation between the individual choices and the
> collective choice obeys certain conditions.
>
> These conditions amount to requiring that every voter's choice has an effect
> not unfavorable to the outcome chosen, and that each voter is less than a
> dictator, yet not wholly powerless.[7]

In particular, we can more clearly specify this in terms of three general
requirements:

First, "if voting for an (outcome) does not produce it, voting for no
other (outcome) will."

Second, "any one voter can be outvoted by the rest together on any
issue."

Third, "every vote (potentially) has some effect on every issue."[8]
Note that this definition of democracy requires that there be some contingencies (i.e., some distributions of choices of others) such that any particular
voter's decision can make a difference, in the desired direction.

[5]Robin Farquharson, *Theory of Voting*, New Haven: Yale University Press, 1969, especially
Chaps. 1 and 2. His concern was not explicitly with democracy as a whole, but rather with the
narrower subject of voting, *per se*. However, his characterization of the context of voting
appears to us to be sufficiently generalizable to constitute an interesting starting point. An
alternative characterization of the context of voting is presented in Douglas W. Rae, Political
Democracy as a Property of Political Institutions," *American Political Science Review*, 65, No. 1,
March 1971, pp. 111–119.

[6]Farquharson, *op. cit.*, p. 5–6.

[7]Farquharson, *op. cit.*, pp. 12–13.

[8]Farquharson, *op. cit.*, p. 13. See his conditions V' and VI'. In a footnote (p. 14),
Farquharson formalizes these conditions in a particularly clear fashion.

Defining democracy in these terms requires that there exist some resource (i.e., votes) that may be cast or not by an individual. An unfortunate limitation of the definition is that the voter cannot choose to divide his votes, or weigh them in some peculiar fashion.[9] Restricted by the first property of the definition, the individual merely can decide (1) whether to cast his votes, and (2) how to cast his votes. This does not exclude other political decisions and other political donations.

Why define democracy in such a broad and technical fashion? Why not simply deal with universal suffrage, one man—one vote rules? If one restricts the definition of democracy to cases involving universal suffrage, for example, it is likely that there will be no real world democracies. What country, city, or state, for instance, allows *everyone* to vote? In the United States, for example, both historically and currently, there are numerous types of disenfranchisement conditions. After the revolution, such things as ancestry, race, sex, and lack of property were sufficient to bar one from voting. Today residency, history of criminal conviction, and the like can cause similar disenfranchisement. Our definition allows us to analyze situations where only a proportion of the people are given the right to vote.

Democracy is defined relative to a group of voters, and not to a political system as a whole. Thus, while for some groups the U. S. Constitution defined a democratic system, for others such as slaves and women, the resulting system was hardly democratic. As written, the Constitution insured that these and other groups were left out of the group of voters. As Congresswoman Jordan has put it:

> "We the people—it is a very eloquent beginning. But when the Constitution of the United States was completed on the 17th of September in 1787, I was not included in that "We the people." I felt for many years that somehow George Washington and Alexander Hamilton just left me out by mistake."[10]

Our definition of democracy will enable us to analyze the workings of the electoral system of the privileged who constituted the voters in the new Republic, just as it enables us to analyze the voting system in a more ideal democracy.

Many normative claims have been made for democracy. Even the modest disclaimer by Churchill that "democracy is the worst form of government, except for all others," is a radical endorsement of the normative aspects of democracy. Clearly, the definition we have established might cover systems that some individuals might find normatively repugnant. But no normative claims for or against democracy are being made here. Instead,

[9]But the definition does not require that each individual have equal votes. Nor does it require that all individuals be given the vote. Every voter must be potentially important but not all individuals need be voters. That is, democracy is defined independently of notions of (1) universal suffrage, (2) one man–one vote notions. Finally, the definition is not restricted to binary procedures: i.e. decisions that are "two-way" races, or motions.

[10]Barbara Jordan, Congresswoman from Texas, 18th district—remarks in a speech to the House Judiciary Committee on articles of impeachment of R. Nixon, July 25, 1974. Note, she was left out twice: once as a woman, and once as a black.

we shall apply the definition to identify characteristics of democracies. In this section of the book we will point out numerous aspects of the relationships between voting and policies, between parties and electorates, between coalitions and preferences, and hence, between ruled and ruler. The theorems that will partially characterize democracy will have normative implications for a balanced evaluation of democracy as a system of group decision making. But these normative implications are not the problem addressed at this time. Rather, given the assumption that voters and politicians are rational, the concern is to characterize the patterns of politics implied by the definition of democracy.

To do this, in Chap. 5, we analyze the act of voting, applying much of the material in Chaps. 2 and 3 to reach our conclusions. In Chap. 6 the question of electoral coalitions will relate to the materials in Chaps. 1 and 4. Here we will reexamine the relationship between the individual's act of voting and the aggregate decisions of the group. We will especially want to examine coalition processes for the types of arbitrariness that we identified in Chap. 1.

II. FOR FURTHER READING

The preceding discussion considered democracy only in its procedural characteristics. Obviously, there are other aspects to democracy which a fuller treatment must take into account. So for example, the liberties which give the procedures meaning involve such things as the relatively uninfringed right to express one's opinion or preferences (and hence, costless voting), the right to introduce new alternatives, etc. For a good discussion of these, and other factors, see Robert Dahl's *Preface to Democratic Theory.* Chicago: Chicago University Press, 1956. But a tension exists between the liberties which give the procedures their appeal and the formal properties of the procedures which we assert make them democratic. Sen[11] proves that even the mildest form of liberalism is incompatible with consistent (i.e. nonarbitrary in the sense of Chapter Two of this volume) democratic decision rules. His result is well worth the pondering of the serious student of liberal democracy.

Besides liberties, Dahl (1956) stresses the egalitarian role ascribed by democracy for each citizen (something we have not built into our definition). Of course, this isn't the only distributive concern contained in modern democratic theory. Equality of opportunity is another aspect of what has long been a distributive element in democratic theory. Those interested in tracing this line of thinking would have to begin with Aristotle's distributive definition of democracy in *Politics,* Book III. A more modern work somewhat in this vein is C. B. Macpherson, *Democratic Theory: Essays in Retrieval,* Oxford: Oxford University Press, 1973.

---

[11]A. K. Sen, *Collective Choice and Social Welfare,* San Francisco: Holden Day, 1970, Chaps. 6 and 6*.

CHAPTER FIVE

VOTING

As defined, voting is a central aspect of democracy, whether the democracy involves only a small group of committee members or a large electorate. Although voting in a small committee may differ in many ways from voting in a large electorate, we begin our analysis of democracy by examining the general characteristics of the act of voting common to either context. Of course, the voter is assumed to be an individual who conforms to our psychological assumptions. That is, voting is an act undertaken to increase expected utility.

The scope of the choice may differ considerably between a committee and an electorate. In a committee, the voting process is explicitly used to create (and adopt) sets of alternatives, while in an electorate, the process is used only to choose between given alternatives. Committees adopt rules and legislation with many possible options and details, all decided upon by complicated series of votes. An electorate usually has a more restricted function: to decide between vaguely and ambiguously defined alternatives. An electorate rarely has more to say about these alternatives than "yea" or "nay."

But the act of voting, in the two cases, still has similarities. Both the committee member and the common citizen is casting a resource within a decision-making system conforming to the definitions of democracy. Although we are concerned here primarily with voting in elections, the reader should consider how much of the analysis is also applicable to acts of voting in other contexts.

I. THE RATIONAL ACT OF VOTING

The theory of the rational act of voting can easily be tied to the previous arguments regarding collective action. Victory of a preferred side in an election can be viewed as a "lumpy" collective good. Donations for such a good can be motivated by either "independent" incentives or by a sufficient probability that the donation will make a difference in the procurement of the good. Thus, in a voting situation, the donor's alternatives, and his calculations regarding them, can be represented in a matrix similar to those presented earlier.

To simplify matters, assume there are only two sides from which to choose. Given the definitions above, the voter either casts his vote for the preferred side or he abstains. This means that he considers only two strategies: voting and nonvoting. Using one row to depict each strategy, the matrix is two rows high. Given the possibility of ties, the voter faces a total of four possible situations depending on the aggregate behavior of others: other votes can aggregate (1) to insure victory for his preferred side; (2) to create a tie in the absence of his vote; (3) to defeat his preferred side by one vote (if he doesn't vote); 4) to insure defeat of his preferred side even if he does vote. These contingencies are represented as four separate columns in a matrix (cf. Table 5–1).

Representing the more preferred side as A, the less preferred side as B, and the individual's cost of voting as C, the value of victory for the preferred side can be written as $U(A-B)$. Define the value of the less desired side as $U(B) = 0$. Recall that the expected value of each outcome is the value of each outcome times the probability of receiving it. Assume that if there is a tie the probability of each side winning is 0.5. Then the expected value for each outcome can be written as follows (assuming that one does not vote):[1]

1. when others' votes insure victory of A: $U(A-B)P_0$;
2. when others' votes lead to tie: $(\frac{1}{2})U(A-B)P_1$;
3. when B wins by one vote: $0P_2$;
4. when B wins by more than one vote: $0P_3$.

Thus, the expected value of not voting (V_0) as an alternative can be expressed as the sum of the expected value of the four outcomes when not voting, as follows:

Table 5-1   The Individual's Decision Matrix Regarding Voting

Amount by which total votes of others fall short of victory for the preferred side	0	1 (tie)	2 (loses by 1)	3 (loses by more than 1)
Probability j assigns to the possibilities that the votes will aggregate as specified	P_0	P_1	P_2	P_3
(Don't vote)	$U(A-B)$	$\frac{1}{2}U(A-B)$*	0	0
(Vote)	$U(A-B)-C$	$U(A-B)-C$	$\frac{1}{2}U(A-B)$*$-C$	$-C$

*The value of a tie is assumed to be equal to one half the value of victory.

[1]Note that here again we assume that it is meaningful to talk about differences in utility numbers, as a utility measure (see Chap. 3).

$$V_0 = U(A-B)P_0 + (\tfrac{1}{2})U(A-B)P_1 + 0(P_2 + P_3) \qquad (5\text{-}1)$$

Similarly, we can symbolize the value of voting as V_D, then:

$$V_D = [U(A-B)](P_0 + P_1) + [\tfrac{1}{2}U(A-B)]P_2 + (-C) \qquad (5\text{-}2)$$

Clearly, if the individual is going to vote, and if he acts according to our behavioral hypotheses, it must be the case that

$$V_D > V_0. \qquad (5\text{-}3)$$

But consider the difference between V_D and V_0. To vote (V_D) involves a cost of C. Aside from this cost, only in the contingencies where the vote makes a difference in the outcome do the payoffs between the two strategies differ. That is, in the two middle columns there is a positive benefit from voting: $\tfrac{1}{2}[U(A-B)]$. To argue that $V_D > V_0$ can be reduced to arguing that:

$$\tfrac{1}{2}[U(A-B)(P_1+P_2)] > C. \qquad (5\text{-}4)$$

That is, in deciding whether or not to vote, the individual must compare the cost of voting with the expected value of actually being the voter who "turned the hand of fate."[2] The value of the difference between the two sides, the probabilities of making a difference, and the cost of voting are the determinants of the rational act of voting. Note that the higher the valuation of the differences between the outcomes $[U(A-B)]$ as compared to the costs of voting, the lower need be the probability that the individual need estimate that his vote will make a difference if he is going to vote.

The politician in search of votes needs to give people an incentive to vote for him.[3] One thing he can do is attempt to lower the cost of voting for his supporters: for example, supply them with transportation to go to the polls. He can increase the differences the individual voters see between the candidates by stressing issue differences between himself and others. And he can co-ordinate individuals' expectations so that they come to believe the election will be very close, and hence, that the probability of a tie is not negligible. These strategic actions can be taken together. If there are

[2]Of course, if one voter makes the difference, then each voter (supporting the winning side) does. A margin of one vote allows each voter to "claim credit" for the victory.

[3]An interesting aside can be made here. If (as in footnote 2) the margin is very small, and any voter can feel very efficacious, then all of them might feel that they played a unique, or special role in the election. This can be a difficulty. Reporting of a city council election won by 40 votes (out of 14,000), Joseph A. Schlesinger writes: "Yet a strange thing began to occur.... when talking to campaign workers and voters it soon became apparent that every one of those voters was one of the last forty and that each worker had brought in the last forty votes. Each appeared to feel, therefore, that he had a special claim. What had happened, clearly enough, was that by achieving a minimum coalition we had maximized the number of marginal voters. And marginal voters, precisely because their votes are the ones needed to win, have a greater claim on the officeholder. Thus, the minimal winning coalition, rather than reducing the number of payoffs which the officeholder had to make, actually appeared to heighten the expectations of payoffs. Perhaps, after all, Downs was right and we should have maximized the vote." "The Primary Goals of Political Parties," *American Political Science Review*, LXIX, No. 3, Sept. 1975, p. 842.

low costs of voting, and very high rewards of victory, the efficacy of the vote need not be as strongly stressed in order to get the individual to make the donation. On the other hand, where the victory is not expected to yield great benefits, the efficacy of the vote must be more strongly stressed, if the voter is to be turned out.

As formulated, one might assert that the theory is too simple. After all, we have excluded how the voter evaluates the alternatives. We have assumed no value accrues from voting, per se. A similar but more complex argument is made by Anthony Downs in his classic work on democracy.[4] His discussion and analysis is richer than our simple model, so let us examine his argument in some detail.

I. THE DOWNSIAN VOTER

The Downsian model of voting rests squarely on the assumption that individual voters are rational. Voters are assumed to evaluate the alternatives and then choose so as to maximize their expected "utility" income.[5] That is, each voter discounts possible benefits and costs by the subjective probabilities associated with their receipt. As discussed in Chap. 3, these discounts are multiplicative.

The Simple Act of Voting

The Downsian voter can choose to vote or to abstain, but he does not determine the alternatives upon which he is to vote. In the event that he chooses to vote, he can decide which party, candidate, or side to support in any given election or referendum. Downs' discussion concerns the factors that the rational voter will take into account in making such choices. Downs assumes the voter restricts his calculations to those potential benefits and costs of voting that are explicitly political. Thus,

> Our approach to elections illustrates how this narrow definition of rationality works. The political function of elections in a democracy, we assume, is to select a government. Therefore, rational behavior in connection with elections is behavior oriented toward this end and no other. Let us assume a certain man prefers party A for political reasons, but his wife has a tantrum whenever he fails to vote for party B. It is perfectly rational *personally* for this man to vote for party B if preventing his wife's tantrums is more important to him than having A win instead of B. Nevertheless, in our model such behavior is considered irrational because it employs a political device for a nonpolitical purpose.[6]

For the Downsian voter: "The benefits voters consider in making their decisions are streams of utility derived from government activity."[7] But the

---

[4]Anthony Downs, *An Economic Theory of Democracy,* New York: Harper and Row, 1957.
[5]See Chap. 3.
[6]Downs, *op. cit.,* p. 7.
[7]*Ibid.,* p. 36.

composition of these utility income streams is somewhat ambiguous. Downs himself is aware that a wide variety of items may play a role in the utility an individual derives from government activity. For example, most people wish to have their streets "policed, water purified, roads repaired, shores defended, garbage removed, weather forecast, etc."[8] This diversity makes it "possible for a citizen to receive utility from events that are only remotely connected to his own material income."[9]

Beyond determining who wins particular political contests, voting plays a second political function. Downs hypothesizes that the utility an individual receives from government is partially a function of the occurrence of elections per se. Moreover:

> Although the benefits each citizen derives from living in a democracy actually accrue to him continuously over time, he can view them as a capital sum which pays interest at each election. This procedure is rational because voting is a necessary prerequisite for democracy; hence democracy is in one sense a reward for voting. We call the part of this reward the citizen receives at each election his *long-run participation value.*
>
> Of course, he will actually get this reward even if he himself does not vote as long as a sufficient number of other citizens do....[10]

For Downs, then, the major rewards from voting spring from two diverse sources: the differences of the alternatives being considered and the preservation of the democratic system. Identifying the source of rewards for the act of voting, however, does not establish the rewards themselves. Consider, for example, the projected rewards of voting for Senator McGovern in the 1972 Presidential election. One might believe that the rewards stem directly from observed differences between the would be programs of McGovern and his opponent (Nixon). But *realized* rewards are not so observable. After all, many voters in 1972 were unable to foresee Nixon's policies accurately. Indeed, this problem is inherent in voting. If one of the candidates is an incumbent, as in the 1972 Presidential election, the voter compares the programs he *expects* the incumbent to carry out over the next election period with the programs he associates with the opposition.

This procedure for comparing parties or candidates exhibits an inherent difficulty: The voter must employ some "rules of thumb" in order to project what candidates or parties are likely to do *once they are in office.* Downs suggests various techniques to deal with this problem, including the use of current performance as an indicator of probable future behavior and reliance upon trend projections.[11] Once these future-oriented judgments of the parties or candidates are made by the voter, the resultant calculations are relatively straightforward, at least when there are only two candidates for a

[8] *Ibid.,* p. 37.
[9] *Ibid.,* p. 37.
[10] *Ibid.,* p. 270.
[11] *Ibid.,* p. 40 *et. seq.*

single office. (In fact, this is the only case for which Downs develops his theory fully.)[12] Thus,

> [E]ach citizen in our model votes for the party he believes will provide him with a higher utility income than any other party during the coming election period.... In a two-party system, this comparison can be set up as a simple subtraction:

$$E(U^A_{t+1}) - E(U^B_{t+1}).$$

> The difference between these two expected utility incomes is the citizen's *expected party differential.*[13]

But the expected party differential is not a sufficient basis for reaching decisions concerning whether to cast a vote or to abstain. After all, each individual voter is aware that his vote is unlikely to make a difference in the outcome of the election. Accordingly, the voter must discount his party differential in some suitable fashion to take into account the small likelihood that his vote will actually change his income stream.

> ... [E]very rational voter realizes that he is not the only person voting. This knowledge radically alters his view of the importance of his own vote.... [H]e must discount his party differential greatly before arriving at the value of voting correctly. This *vote value* is compounded from his estimates of his party differential and of the probability that his vote will be decisive.[14]

Under the circumstances, the value to any given individual of casting a vote (as opposed to abstaining) is extremely small, and it varies as a function of those factors which determine the likelihood of his vote making a difference.

In summary, Downs' expected party differential is composed of conjectured future performance differences between the parties discounted by the probability of a vote making a difference. The resultant discounted difference, measured in terms of utility income, constitutes the total benefit obtainable from voting when voting is merely a means of determining the outcome of the contest at hand. However, to this must be added the consequences of casting a vote for the perpetuation of the democratic system.

---

[12]The difficulty with the calculations when there are more than two candidates is that the individual may have an incentive to vote for a candidate who is not his most preferred. He might do this, for example, if his most preferred candidate was likely to be the smallest getter of votes, whereas his second choice candidate had a good chance of winning. This is discussed in Downs, *op. cit.,* pp. 146–154. Such a voting strategy is usually referred to as "strategic voting." The reader interested in pursuing the topic further should see Robin Farquharson's classic *Theory of Voting,* New Haven: Yale University Press, 1969. On another formulation of the problem of rational voting with more than two candidates, see John A. Ferejohn and Morris P. Fiorina, "The Paradox of Not Voting: A Decision Theoretic Analysis," *American Political Science Review,* V. 68, No. 2, June 1974, pp. 525–536.

[13]Downs, *op. cit.,* p. 39. In this formulation, t+1 is the period of incumbency of the government to be elected, $E(U)$ symbolizes the expected value of U, and U^A and U^B are the utility streams flowing from the alternative governments.

[14]*Ibid.,* p. 244.

Thus, the total return which a rational citizen receives from voting in a given election consists of his long-run participation value plus his discounted party differential. . . .[15]

The rational individual must compare this total return or benefit associated with voting with his estimate of the cost of voting. If the estimated cost of voting is less than the expected benefits, the individual will go to the polls and cast a vote. On the other hand, if the estimated cost exceeds the expected benefits, he will abstain from voting. This formula is usually sufficient to guide the voting behavior of the rational individual. However, it is possible for the value of an individual's vote to be greater than his estimated cost of voting, even though he perceives no significant differences between the parties. This would be due to his "long-run participation value." Downs assumes that such individuals will actually vote, although their choice of one candidate or another will be random.

In summary, we can develop two major conjectures:

> *The voter will abstain from voting if and only if the costs of voting outweigh the benefits from voting.*

In a two-way race:

> *The voter will support that party or candidate which he prefers.*

These conjectures, at least when properly fleshed out by Downs, admit of testing. Given the wealth of voting studies, it would be interesting to see how the theory fares in light of the data.

II. TESTING THE DOWNSIAN THEORY OF VOTING

Ideally, any test of a theory should be based on data that conforms with the situational limitations of the theory itself. For example, the Downsian theory of voting is developed for situations in which the voter is going to the polls to vote in a single election, not a multitude of electoral contests. But in the United States most election days are the time when a multitude of elections are decided. One goes to the polls once, but one casts many votes. For example, one may cast a vote for President, congressman, governor, state senator, and mayor on the same day. Thus, a voter might be motivated to go to the polls in order to cast a vote in the congressional race, but once at the polls, he finds he is willing to indicate preferences in the other races. Or it may be that no one race is sufficient incentive to go to the polls, but the collection of races, in the aggregate, gives sufficient payoffs from voting to attract the individual to the polls. This means that data collected regarding voting in the United States must be collected in situations where there is simultaneous voting in numerous races. Of course, this merely illustrates a more general problem: There are gaps between the characteristics of situations that are the source of data and the situations theoretically de-

---

[15] *Ibid.*, p. 270.

scribed. These gaps should be remembered in any evaluation of the data presented below.

With this caveat, let us note that the theory would predict that:

> Individuals who find either strong differences between candidates in an extremely close race (i.e. a relatively high probability that every vote will count), or that democracy is important to their well being, will be more likely to turn out to vote than individuals who find that (A) either the differences between candidates are unimportant, or the race is one-sided (and hence one's vote is unlikely to make any difference), and (B) that the democratic system or group decision has not led to personal benefits.

The set of hypotheses embodied in this statement was tested by the use of data from the Presidential elections of 1952–1960 and the results were reported by William Riker and Peter Ordeshook. The theory is well supported by the data. In particular, the Downsian model makes 20 independent conjectures regarding turnout, as a function of party differential, citizen duty, and perceived closeness of the electoral contest, when data is reported as in Table 5–2. The predictions are specified in part *a* of Table

Table 5-2   Voter Turnout and Voter Rationality: Theory and Data—

a. *Theoretical Predictions*

Expected closeness of election result	High		Medium		Low	
	High P.D.	Low P.D.	High P.D.	Low P.D.	High P.D.	Low P.D.
close	a	c	e	g	i	k
not close	b	d	f	h	j	l

(P.D. = Party differential)
Predicted relationships (independent):
 Turnout higher if election perceived to be close:
  $a > b, c > d, e > f, g > h, i > j, k > l$;
 Turnout higher if party differential is higher:
  $a > c, b > d, e > g, f > h, i > k, j > l$;
 Turnout higher if 'Citizen Duty' score is higher:
  $a > e > i, d > h > l, c > g > k, b > f > j$

b. *1952-1960 Presidential Election Data:*[*]

Expected closeness of election result	High		Medium		Low	
	High P.D.	Low P.D.	High P.D.	Low P.D.	High P.D.	Low P.D.
close	91%	83%	85%	71%	63%	44%
not close	86%	74%	77%	71%	62%	39%

'Citizen Duty Score'

(P.D. = party differential, i.e. how much difference the respondent thought it made which side won)
The percentages give the proportion who voted in each category. Calculated from Riker, 1968, Table 3, page 38.

[*] As summarized by Brian M. Barry, *Sociologists, Economists and Democracy*, London: Collier-Macmillan, 1970, p. 17. The original reporting of this data was by Riker and Ordeshook, "A Theory of the Calculus of Voting," *American Political Science Review*, LXII, No. 1, March 1968, p. 38.

5–2 and are strictly "ordinal." Note that all but one of 20 predictions ($g > h$ predicted but $g = h$ in the data) are borne out by the data in part b of Table 5–2. Note also that, as Brian Barry has said regarding this data,

> There is clearly an interaction effect among two of the variables: when "citizen duty" is medium or high, "party differential" makes only a modest difference to voting levels, but among those with a low score on "citizen duty" (who presumably have little reason to vote just for the sake of voting) "party differential" makes a difference of around twenty percentage points.[16]

That is, party differences make more difference when there is little other reason to vote. Precisely what Downs would predict.[17]

The findings reported in Table 5–3 further corroborate the rational voter hypotheses. These findings were based on surveys done by the Survey Research Center. The authors of the surveys have broken down the statistics for the 1956 election in ways that perhaps measure, in a different way, the three variables already related in Table 5–2. Once again, the data supports the theory.

In the first table (5–3a), concern over election outcome is a more generalized measure than party differential. As predicted, as concern over outcome increases, so does turnout. Similarly, in Table 5–3b, sense of political efficacy is not based on closeness of election but rather on the individual's perception of the 'power of the common citizen to affect the government' by his or her individual actions. In this case if we assume that the more general feelings of efficacy hold also for the efficacy of voting, a prediction can be made: as efficacy increases, so does turnout. The pre-

[16]Barry, *op. cit.*, p. 18. Barry's book consists of a careful contrast of Downs' theory with a more "sociological" theory of voting.

[17]On the other hand, even in the lower left hand corner of the table, where voters who have little sense of duty to vote, perceptions of only small differences between the candidates, and feel that their vote is unlikely to make any difference, 39% of these individuals vote. Also note that we are assuming that even in a large electorate (i.e. about 50–70 million) individuals perceive *some* probability that their vote will make a difference. And this probability is not infinitesimal. Indeed, Barry views this as a major weakness of the theory:

> "Riker suggests that electors may hold grossly inflated notions of their chances of altering the result, based on the occasional dramatic case, and that their party differentials may be far higher than is normally supposed (Riker, *op. cit.*, pages 38–9). This seems to me a pretty desperate salvage attempt." Barry, *op. cit.*, p. 18.

An alternative explanation for the rationality of voting, one which avoids this problem, is contained in John A. Ferejohn and Morris P. Fiorina, *American Political Science Review op. cit.*, p. 525. Their analysis is based on the maximin regret principle of rational decision making under uncertainty; see Chap. 3, above, for a discussion of this alternative to the maximization of expected utility hypothesis. Their argument would appear to explain why many individuals turn out in an election. But they would have difficulty explaining why so few turn out (13%) when one considers only those individuals who do not appear to be motivated by "citizen duty," c.f. Table 5–3c.

Finally, given the subjective scales involved, another view is suggested by Norman Frohlich, Joe Oppenheimer, Jeffery Smith, and Oran Young, "A Test of Downsian Voter Rationality: 1964 Presidential Voting," *American Political Science Review*, forthcoming.

dicted relationship is supported by the data. Finally, Table 5–3 indicates that as sense of duty increases, so does turnout.

In these results, the number of individuals who vote in spite of no apparent incentive is significantly lower than the residual percentage of voters who appeared to vote without reason in Table 5–2. On the other hand, there still are some "unexplained" voters. Similarly, there are some voters who appear to have a very high incentive to turn out who do not do so. Both residual groups can, perhaps, "be explained away," but without systematic analysis of these voters, they should be viewed as deviant cases.

There are other less direct indicators that we can use to "test" the rationality of voters. For example, in measuring the individual's preference of one party over another, the Survey Research Center uses a number of different indicators. These indicators resulted, for some individuals, in cross-pressured patterns of preference. That is, some individuals were shown to have Democratic leanings along some dimensions and Republican leanings along others. If voters are rational, these cross pressures would tend to offset one another. Thus, more cross-pressured individuals would have a smaller concern regarding the outcome of the election than those exhibiting less cross pressure. Of course, all dimensions might not be

Table 5-3   Turnout and Concern Over Election Outcome, Sense of Political Efficacy and Citizen Duty*

(a) *Relation of Degree of Concern About Election Outcome to Voting Turnout, 1956*

	Degree of Concern over Election Outcome			
	Don't Care at All	*Don't Care Very Much*	*Care Somewhat*	*Care Very Much*
Voted	52%	69%	76%	84%
Did not vote	48	31	24	16
Number of cases	230	367	627	459

(b) *Relation of Sense of Political Efficacy to Voting Turnout, 1956*

	Sense of Political Efficacy				
	Low				*High*
Voted	52%	60%	75%	84%	91%
Did not vote	48	40	25	16	9
Number of cases	263	343	461	501	196

(c) *Relation of Sense of Citizen Duty to Voting Turnout, 1956*

	Low				High
	Low				*High*
Voted	13%	42%	52%	74%	85%
Did not vote	87	58	48	26	15
Number of cases	89	78	146	639	812

*Angus Campbell, et al. *The American Voter: An Abridgement,* New York: Wiley, 1964, pp. 57–59.

equally important, but the survey did not tap this possibility. Thus the argument can only be made probabilistically: the higher the conflict, the less the probability that the individual cared about the outcome of the election. The results confirm this hypothesis. Note, in Figure 5-1, the greater the conflict (i.e. toward the middle of the horizontal scale), the higher the percentage of individuals not caring about the outcome.

These data constitute substantial support for the assumption of voter rationality in the American electorate. The relationships are on the whole in the direction predicted. Even the residual "outliers," i.e. those with little motivation who do vote, and those with great motivation who don't vote, are not numerous, nor inherently falsifying cases. With this positive result, it is useful to extend the theoretical analysis beyond the simple original formulation of who votes and for whom.

III. RATIONAL IGNORANCE

One obvious characteristic of most voting decisions is that the individual has a very low probability of making a difference. Thus, the expected value of the act of voting is likely to be very low. As already argued, it would be irrational to spend a great deal of effort on voting. Analogously, it would be irrational for most voters to put forth a great deal of effort to get information about the issues and candidates, to become a "well-informed" voter.

In other words, given the low probability that voting will make any difference to the voter, the act of voting is, in most situations, a relatively unimportant event in an individual's life. Thus, often it will be irrational to acquire the information needed in order to make informed decisions concerning voting. The costs of becoming informed about the details of the issue components of the party differential are apt to be far greater than the benefits an individual can expect to gain from voting on an "informed" (rather than an "uninformed") basis. After all, the *benefits* of voting on an informed basis can't be more than the *discounted* difference between the voter's valuation of the candidate one eventually votes for and the candidate one would have voted for if one remained uninformed.[18] And the *costs* of being informed *are not similarly discounted.* Downs has distinguished three different sorts of cost involved in becoming informed:

    a. *Procurement costs* are the costs of gathering, selecting, and transmitting data.
    b. *Analysis costs* are the costs of making factual analysis of data.
    c. *Evaluative costs* are the costs of relating data or factual analyses to specific goals; i.e. of evaluating them.[19]

[18]Perhaps it would be useful to sketch the steps in this argument. Information is assumed to be only instrumentally useful. Thus, it is only "worthwhile" when it stops you from doing something you were going to do before you had the information. In other words being better informed is only valuable if it changes the action chosen. Thus, the value of the information can not be greater than the difference in the expected value of the strategies being compared.

[19]Downs, *op. cit.,* p. 210, italics in the original. Note that an individual's costs will be determined by such factors as education, job, etc.

But as Downs pointed out, many of the costs can be transferred to others who may be willing to bear them. Furthermore under the circumstances, rational voters will often wish to develop methods of avoiding the costs of information acquisition. That is, the voter seeks shortcuts in the gathering of information. It follows that political competitors must appeal to voters who are not particularly interested in obtaining information.

These arguments concerning reasons why voters may find it rational to remain at least partially uninformed lead Downs to describe different types of voters in the following fashion:

> . . . some rational men habitually vote for the same party in every election. In several preceding elections, they carefully informed themselves about all the competing parties, and all the issues of the moment; yet they always came to the same decision about how to vote. Therefore they have resolved to repeat this decision automatically without becoming well-informed, unless some catastrophe makes them realize it no longer expresses their best interests. Like

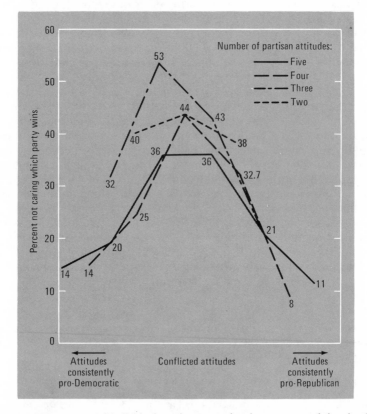

Figure 5-1   Cross pressured individuals and concern for the outcome of the election
*Campbell et al. *op. cit.*, p. 47.

all habits, this one saves resources, since it keeps voters from investing in information which would not alter their behavior. Thus it is a rational habit.[20]

The conclusion is clear:

Voters will often find it rational to remain relatively ignorant.

Therefore, we would expect many individuals to develop long-term party identifications with one party or another. They vote for their preferred party's candidates during any election. This pattern would break down for the more informed voter when his information indicates that his party loyalty is not consistent with current issue differences between the parties. Then, the more solid an individual feels is his information about the current issues, the more likely he would be to override his traditional party loyalty. Looking at individuals "whose attitudes toward the current elements of politics contradict their sense of party identification," we find exactly this. In Table 5–4 we examine voters whose preferred party is taking a stand against the voter's preferences on some issue. And the more developed the voter's policy ideas, the more likely he is to vote against his preferred party.

Table 5–4   Party Identification and Voter Willingness to Override It on the Basis of Further Information*

Relation of Degree of Attitude Development to Direction in Which Conflict of Party Identification and Partisan Evaluations Is Resolved in Voting[a]

	Those Who Have Formed Evaluations		Those Who Have Formed No Evaluations at All
	That Are Well-Developed	That Are Poorly Developed	
Vote agrees with party identification	20%	47%	75%
Vote fails to agree with party identification	80	53	25
Number of cases	143	164	36

[a] Figures in this table are based on a combination of data from the 1952 and 1956 election samples.
*Campbell, et. al. *op. cit.*, p. 82.

IV. FOR WHOM IS IT RATIONAL TO BE MORE INFORMED?

Noting that some voters have well developed policy preferences raises the question of when, and on what issues, voters will make the effort to get information and develop positions. The obvious conclusion is that voters

[20]Downs, *op. cit.*, p. 100.

will be most likely to be informed regarding issues that are of major importance to their overall well-being. Moreover, when parties take different stands on issues of major importance to an identifiable and organized group, we would expect to find these differences reflected in the votes of the groups. For even if the individual feels that there is no chance of affecting the outcome of the election, the voter is also part of an organized group. By voting in accordance with his group's position, he is contributing to the group's ability to collectively bring pressure on future candidates.

Indirect confirmation of these hypotheses is given by data on the behavior of Jews, blacks, and farmers. As might be expected, an issue of major concern to farmers is the state of the economy as it relates to the prices that they receive for their particular crops. Rises in the prices they receive for their crops should be translatable into support for the incumbent administration, and similarly declines in prices should be reflected in support for a change.

Table 5–5 illustrates the point by showing that farmers voted for a change in the White House in apparent response to the prices they received for their crops. Furthermore, small farmers, who would be more likely to be affected by short-run price fluctuations are found to be more affected in their vote as a function of price changes for their crops than are large farmers. The trend in prices for agricultural products is an area in which the farmer is apparently informed,[21] and an area that affects the voting decision.

Issues of equivalent importance to other groups have often emerged in the American electoral arena. For American Jews, the rise of Nazi dicta-

Table 5–5   Important Issues and Party Choice: Farmers and Prices*

Relation of Trend of Prices Received by the Farmer, 1952–1956, to His 1956 Vote

	Reported Price Trend		
	Up a Little; Same; or Mixed Trends Balancing Out	Down a Little	Down a Lot
Proportion voting Democratic	13%	39%	66%
Number of cases	27	36	29

Relation of Farm Price Trends and Farm Size to 1956 Presidential Vote of Farmers

	Southern Small Farm		Southern Large Farm		Non-Southern Small Farm		Non-Southern Large Farm	
Prices are . . .	Down	Up or Same	Down	Up or Same	Down	Up or Same	Down	Up or Same
Proportion voting Democratic	100%	55%	70%	50%	62%	33%	41%	6%
Number of cases	9	11	10	10	26	9	37	17

*Campbell, et al., *op. cit.*, p. 219.

[21]Note that this information is obtained quite freely as a result of the farmer's work. His application of the information to politics is, presumably, costless.

torship in Germany and the American response to it can be viewed as such an issue.[22] The issue of governmental support programs for disadvantaged groups (e.g. blacks) during the depression and the voting patterns of these groups can be analyzed similarly. In the face of such important issues we could expect informed and organized voters to use their information to re-evaluate any previous ("cost-saving") habits of voting and party identifications. Where party identification and informed preferences on issues positions contradicted one another, the assumption of rationality would predict that voters would vote the issues and not their prior allegiances. A description of shifts in the voting patterns of American Jews and blacks indicates exactly that shift:

The Jewish minority comprises one of the most Democratic groups to be found in the electorate; Democratic Jews outnumber Republican Jews in the order of 4-1. During the 1920's the vote in heavily Jewish districts of the Eastern metropolises ran as high as 80 per cent Republican. Although vote is not the same as party identification, it can scarcely be doubted that the orientation of this group toward the two parties was substantially altered during the 1930's. We may surmise that the rise of the Nazi dictatorship in Germany and the opposition of the Roosevelt Administration to it must have played an important role in this change. Whatever the cause, the shift of Jewish allegiances to the Democratic Party was one of the most impressive of the several group movements in political preference during the Roosevelt period.

Prior to the 1930's, so far as we can tell from election statistics, the prevailing political preference among Negroes was Republican. This was a consequence, of course, of the Civil War and the attachment of Negroes to the party of Lincoln. During the 1930's politics took on a different significance to the Negro tenth of the electorate. It is impossible to know whether the shift of Negro allegiances to the Democratic standard from the traditions inherited from earlier generations occurred as the reactions of individual Negroes to the personalities and events of the times or as a mass movement resulting largely from the mobilization of Negro senitment by an articulate leadership. No doubt both of these circumstances were present. In any case, the conversion of Negroes to the Democratic Party was very substantial. During the Eisenhower period Democratically identified Negroes outnumbered Republican Negroes by a margin of 3-1.[23]

The evidence is suggestive, though not conclusive. More imaginative and elaborate tests have been conducted, but of course, evidence cannot establish the theory beyond doubt. Rather, it should be viewed as a basis for establishing the credibility of the conjectures, to be juxtaposed against the performance of the models under more rigorous tests yet to be designed.

[22]Again, for most Jews accurate information on this issue would have been gathered in talking to relatives, etc. Thus the information was "costlessly" available for political application.
[23]Campbell, *et al., op. cit.,* pp. 92-3.

V. FORMS OF CONTRIBUTION AND PARTICIPATION OTHER THAN VOTING

Although voting may be a defining characteristic of democracy, voting is virtually never the *only* means of affecting the outcome of political contests. It is a cheap means and it may be available to almost everyone. But because so many can vote an individual's vote is unlikely to affect the outcome of any particular election. Thus we have concluded that often it is rational to stay ignorant. Often contributions other than votes have a greater chance of affecting the electoral outcome than do votes themselves. Money spent on campaign advertising, or time spent canvassing, etc. for one candidate or another is likely to affect the actions of a number of voters. Such donations as time and money are likely to involve a greater sacrifice than mere voting. But the probability of such a donation making a difference is bigger.

Other Contributions and Information

We would expect that if individuals are rational, they would be more likely to become informed before making a large contribution than before making a small one. They would also be more likely to become informed before making a relatively effective contribution than a relatively ineffective one. After all, good information can save them the cost of making the costly contribution, and it can also insure that the possible gains from the act of contributing are protected from error.

Thus, contributors of money can be expected to be more informed, politically, than the average voter. And large contributors have reasons to be quite well informed. Although we know of no direct tests of this hypothesis, there are ways of testing the hypothesis indirectly. Given "objective" differences between the parties in the United States, the large contributors of money would tend to agree on these differences. This agreement should be identifiable by the same sort of "bloc voting" with dollars as we would predict for individuals with similar interests who merely cast votes. Thus, for example, we have already noted the "bloc voting" patterns of voters. Voters in the same bloc seem to agree on differences between parties. If these differences do exist, and if the voter is less informed than the large contributor, even tighter bloc patterns will emerge with dollars than with votes. What is the evidence?

It would be best to have information on monetary donations about the same groups as we have for voters. But this data is not always available. Instead, we can employ the strength of bloc voting among Jews, blacks, and union members as indicators of maximum cohesion among voting blocs in the United States. Of course, the theory predicts that individuals who more strongly identify themselves with these groups will vote more strongly in accordance with these bloc patterns. Since the New Deal, all three of these blocs identify their interests with policy positions of the Democratic party; therefore, we can measure their bloc solidarity by the percentage of Democratic voters in each group (see Table 5–6). Of these three groups, we can compare only the "bloc" donation of money from union members with the "bloc" voting characteristics of members of union households. Imperfect as

Table 5-6   Bloc Voting Patterns for Selected Groups With High Solidarity*

Vote Division Within Four Test Groups, According to Strength of Group Identification, 1956ᵃ

	Highly Identified	Weakly Identified	Discrepancy
Members of union households	64	36	+28
Catholics	51	39	+11
Negroes			
Non-South	72	63	+9
South	.. b	.. b	.. b
Jews	83	55	+28

ᵃThe entries in the first two columns represent the per cent Democratic of the two-party vote division. The final column summarizes the differences between percentages in the first two, a plus indicating that high identifiers in the group voted more strongly Democratic.
ᵇSouthern Negro voters in the sample are too few for further subdivision.

Distinctiveness of Presidential Vote among Certain Groups, with Life Situation Controlled, 1956ᵃ

Members of union households	+17.1
Union members	+20.4
Catholics	+ 2.9
Negroes	
Non-South	+11.6
South	+15.4
Jews	+45.4

ᵃThe entry in each cell represents a deviation in per cent Democratic of the two-party vote within the test group from a comparable per cent computed for control groups matched with the tes groups for a variety of conditions of life situation.
*Campbell, et. al., *op. cit.*, p. 167, 169.

these comparisons may be, they are at least indirect indications of the differences in the information levels of voters and monetary donors. While voters who were labor union members split 2-1 pro Democratic party, labor money split more than 250-1 for the Democratic party.[24] As Campbell, *et al.* report in the quote above, few groups—if any—show greater voting solidarity than the Jews. They vote in blocs with 80 percent of the individuals staying with the Democrats. Yet numerous groups contribute money with far greater solidarity than that. For example, consider defense contractors, whose money split 86 percent for the Republicans, or the contributions of the wealthiest Americans which split 93 percent for the Republicans during the 1968 campaign.[25] Neither of these groups may have quite the 'issue agreement' or solidarity of interests that marked unions when it comes to partisan preference. If, however, we examine more identifiable interest clus-

[24]Out of more than $1,000,000 contributed by 155 state and local labor groups in 1956, to all candidates for Federal office, only $3,925 went to Republicans. See Alexander Heard, *Costs of Democracy*, p. 186–87.
[25]*Dollar Politics, The Issue of Campaign Spending*, Vol. 1, Washington D.C.: Congressional Quarterly Research Staff, 1971, p. 36. If one notes that some contributors donated to both parties (perhaps for different candidates), and only considers those who donated to only one party, the money went 98 percent for the Republicans. *Ibid.*, p. 33.

ters, we find greater solidarity. Among 30 members of the American Iron and Steel Institute (an industry association) who each contributed over $500 to political campaigns between 1952 and 1956, all gave only to the Republican party. Similarly, the 82 members of the American Petroleum Institute giving over $500 included two individuals who donated to both parties, one who gave to the Democrats and 79 who gave to the Republicans. The twenty-four $500 contributors in the National Coal Association unanimously chose the Republicans. Indeed, such donors from business groups checked by Heard seemed to favor Republicans about 49–1.[26]

Thus the rationality of ignorance can be contrasted with the rationality of being informed:

> *Individuals contemplating costly and effective donations have greater incentives to be informed than the average voter.*

Note that the above argument did not assume that the larger donors were requesting favors, or changes in programs from the candidates. If we allow for such favors, or purchases, we would expect even greater reasons for individuals to be well informed, especially in areas of immediate impact on their incomes. Thus, as Downs puts it:

> Naturally, the men who stand most to gain from exerting influence in a policy area are the ones who can best afford the expense to becoming expert about it. Their potential returns from influence are high enough to justify a large investment of information. In almost every policy area, those who stand the most to gain are the men who earn their incomes there. This is true because most men earn their incomes in one area but spend them in many; hence the area of earning is much more vital to them than any one area of spending.[27]

Independent Incentives

Often contributions made in politics are in direct exchange for some favor. There are indirect tests to see whether contributions are being made for favors. When individuals consider contributing for the victory of a preferred candidate, the closer the anticipated contest, the greater the incentive to contribute. Taking action is predicated on being able to make a difference. Thus, if one candidate were a *sure* winner, citizens would not contribute to increase his chances of victory. If a citizen contributes to a campaign fund *after* the election, and after the candidate has announced that he or she has a surplus, the contribution is not being made to insure victory. The most reasonable conclusion to draw is that the contribution was made to gain some particular favor. A similar observation could be made of individuals who contribute to both sides of a political contest. Again the contribution is not being made to increase the odds of victory for the preferred candidate. Thus, when Ruth Farkas paid two-thirds of her $300,000 contribution to Richard Nixon's 1972 election committee after the election and after a

[26]See Heard, *op. cit.*, pp. 100–102.
[27]Downs, *op. cit.*, p. 254.

surplus in his campaign fund had been declared, it is not unreasonable to assume that she did it to get the ambassadorship to Luxembourg.

These observations can be generalized. In electoral campaigns when individuals are contributing primarily to increase the probability of victory of their preferred candidate, if the contest begins to look too one sided, their incentive to act is diminished. Regarding actions to insure victory, politicians can "peak" too early. To attract contributions based on these motives, successful politicians can always be expected to "run scared." They will discount reports of one-sided victories in the making, at least among their supporters. On the other hand, if votes or contributions are being made to secure favors from a candidate, then as he is approaching, or secures, the victory, contributors can be expected to rush to his side in a stampede. In order to insure that they get their favor they must deliver their support while it is still valued by the candidate. If the candidate is successful before the contributor has made his move, the contributor's resources are devalued and the favors he can command are diminished. Thus, genuine bandwagon effects in an election can be expected in situations in which the contributors expect favors in exchange for their support. Peaking is to be expected regarding the voting of the general populus in general elections. Bandwagoning is predictable among the special interest lobbies and in arenas like presidential nominating conventions.[28] Close elections will similarly lead favor seekers to contribute to both sides.

The possibility of other forms of contribution raise questions regarding the effect of the distribution of resources other than votes on the outcomes of voting processes. This question is, in the main, beyond the scope of this volume although some relevant material is developed in the next chapter. Having examined at least some aspects of the behavior of individuals in a democratic context, let us turn to the question of what the systemic effects of such behavior are likely to be. In a democracy what can we expect of the government's policies and their relationships with the voters' preferences?

VI. FOR FURTHER READING

Aside from the material already alluded to, there is a voluminous literature on voting and electoral behavior. Perhaps most significant of the pieces not identified previously is the long exchange on the 1972 Presidential Election over the article by Miller, et al. "A Majority Party in Disarray," all in the *American Political Science Review*, LXX, September 1976, No. 3., pp. 753–849. Special attention should be directed to the "Comment" by Samuel Popkin, et al. But a major other work to be examined is John Kingdon's, *Candidates for Office*, New York: Random House, 1968. An enjoyable and well argued criticism of the "rational voter perspective" is Paul E. Meehl, "The Selfish

[28]For a slightly more elaborated discussion of this point see Norman Frohlich; *et al. Political Leadership and Collective Goods*, Princeton, N.J.: Princeton University Press, 1970, pp. 108–114.

Voter Paradox and the Thrown Away Vote Argument," *American Political Science Review*, LXXI, March 1977, No. 1, pp. 11–30.

For material on the financing of the electoral process in the U.S., the interested reader should consult the very fine works sponsored by the Congressional Quarterly. See their *Dollar Politics*, Volumes 1 and 2, Washington, D.C.: 1971 and 1974. Also examine the comprehensive work on the subject by Herbert E. Alexander, *Financing Politics: Money, Elections and Political Reform*, Washington, D.C.: Congressional Quarterly, 1976. An interesting review of these (and other) works on money and politics is David Adamany, "Money, Politics, and Democracy," *American Political Science Review*, LXXI, March 1977, No. 1, pp. 289–304.

On the effects of rational ignorance, and how this can lead to difficulties for the theory of democracy, see Isaac D. Balbus, "The Concept of Interest in Pluralist and Marxian Analysis," *Politics and Society*, Vol. I, 2, February 1971, pp. 151–177. The potential for the manipulation of interests, given the incentive for ignorance on the part of the voter, is clear. To illustrate, the reader might find a work such as Stanley Kelley, Jr., *Professional Public Relations and Political Power*, Baltimore: Hopkins, 1956 more revealing than some of the newer works more oriented toward the persuasive powers of television.

PARTY PLATFORMS
IN A DEMOCRACY

From the previous chapter we know that in order to attract voters politicians will manipulate their policy positions and platforms. The rational politician interested in winning will construct a set of policy positions with the voters' preferences in mind designed to capture a majority of the votes. But given the problem of cyclical majorities (the voters' paradox) and Arrow's Impossibility Theorem (cf. Chap. 2) there is clearly no guarantee that any one set of policy positions can gain a majority against *all* other sets. It would be astonishing to discover that all political competitions miraculously escape the problems posed by cyclical patterns of group preferences. Thus, at least some of the time, the set of policy positions pieced together by each of the political competitors will have the unhappy property of being beatable by another platform.

Of course, there are also situations in which no preference cycles occur. In such cases, one set of policy positions (or candidate and associated positions) will be capable of getting a majority against all other positions (no matter how the agenda is set). Such a motion would be chosen by majoritarian rule in pairwise voting and would emerge as the unequivocal winner. Any "motion" or candidate or set of policy positions with this characteristic is referred to as a *Condorcet winner*. It can defeat all others in pairwise votes.

But what if there is no Condorcet winner, no unequivocally "first" group choice? What are the characteristics of individual preference patterns

---

[1]A most interesting and nontechnical discussion of the characteristics of a Condorcet winner may be found in Duncan Black, *The Theory of Committees and Elections*, Cambridge: 1958, Chaps. 9 and 18. In Chap. 9, Black compares the normative qualities of choosing such a motion with the choice of motions having other characteristics. In Chap. 18, he considers the historical development of the concept of a Condorcet winner. For a brief introduction to the concept of a Condorcet winner, see William Riker and Peter Ordeshook, *An Introduction to Positive Political Theory*, Englewood Cliffs, New Jersey: Prentice Hall, 1973, p. 89.

that do, and do not, yield Condorcet winners? When does the possibility of a voters' paradox exist? To examine these conditions, we will begin by looking at one condition: single-peaked preferences (identified in Chap. 1). As was previously pointed out single-peaked preferences guarantee a Condorcet winner. We will develop some of the theoretical and empirical applications and limitations of this, and related, notions.

I. SINGLE-PEAKED PREFERENCES WITH ONE ISSUE

If only one issue is at stake and the preferences of the individuals are single-peaked over that issue, Black has demonstrated that the preferred position of the median voter can beat any other position. The preference of the median voter is, therefore, a Condorcet winner.[2]

To see how his conclusions follow, consider again the characteristics of single-peaked preferences. By definition, single-peaked preferences require that there exist some ordering of all proposals so that each individual's preferences fall off (not necessarily uniformly) in either direction as one moves away from his most preferred point. For some issues, such a configuration of preferences seems quite reasonable. For example, consider the size of a budget for improvements in a local park. It seems plausible that each individual could specify his (or her) optimum in dollars. In Figure 6–1, the horizontal axis represents the total feasible range of the improvement budget. The vertical axis represents the preference order of the individuals. That is, a point at a given height is preferred to all points below it. Thus, an individual's most preferred point (or optimum) will be the highest peak in his preference curve. In the figure, Ms. S's preferences indicate O_S to be her optimum. As one moves from her optimum (either to the left or the right), the motions are continuously less desirable. Her preferences are, therefore, single peaked. An example of a *non*single-peaked preference is that of Mr. Q. Moving to the right from his optimum (O_Q) to point A, his preferences decline, but from A to B they increase again, thus creating a "second peak" (at B) in his preference function. Black's theorem is: *if all voters have preferences that are single peaked the median optimum will be the Condorcet winner.*

To see this for the case of an odd number of voters is relatively simple. Consider a set of voters (of odd number $= n$) with single-peaked preferences given a particular ordering along one dimension of the propositions to be voted upon. Let O_{med} be the median optimum. This definition of O_{med} insures that there are an equal number of voters with optima to the

[2]Duncan Black, "On the Rationale of Group Decision Making," *Journal of Political Economy*, **56**, 1948, pp. 23–24 and "The Decisions of a Committee Using a Special Majority," *Econometrica*, 16, 1948, pp. 245–261. (And in *The Theory of Committees and Elections*, pp. 14–18.) If the number of voters is even "the median positions" would tie; if the number is odd the single median would win. An accessible alternative presentation is available in R. Duncan Luce and Howard Raiffa, *Games and Decisions*, New York: Wiley, 1957, pp. 353–357.

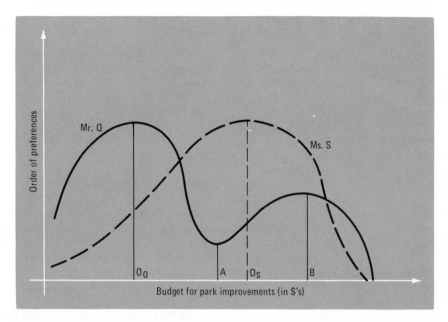

Figure 6–1   Single-peaked and multipeaked preferences.

left and to the right of O_{med}: $\frac{n-1}{2}$ voters on either side. Consider a contest between O_{med} and any alternative (O') to the left of O_{med}: $\frac{n-1}{2}$ voters have preferences to the right of O_{med}, and for each of them both O_{med} and O' are to the left of their optima. But for each of them, O_{med} is closer than O', and they all prefer the closer to the more distant point: O_{med} to O'. Of course, the voter with the median optimum prefers O_{med} to anything (and hence to O'). Thus, O_{med} is guaranteed *at least* a bare majority against any alternative to the left of it. Similarly it is guaranteed at least a majority against any alternative to the right of it. Thus it is a guaranteed winner against any alternative.

Given the strength of the theorem, it becomes interesting to consider what sorts of electoral contests and voting situations can be expected to involve single-peaked preferences along one dimension. Typically, such situations should involve a single issue characterized by a single aspect that is salient and measurable (at least in ordinal terms) by everyone. An election based on the *size* of the budget, say for a school board (or any other functional unit of government), is an example of a contest in which the single-peaked assumptions may be applicable. From this, we can predict that if two candidates for a school-board position campaign on the issue of the size of the budget, both might aim for that budget size representing the optimum of the median voter. Because of the stability of the median optima as a Condorcet winner, the strategic choice of which issue positions to adopt can be analyzed using the single-peaked notions developed by Black.

II. ELECTORAL COMPETITION AS "SPATIAL" COMPETITION

It is not a great leap from the notion of an underlying ordering of the alternatives to the notion of a one-dimensional "issue space." Indeed, as far back as 1929, at least one analyst, Harold Hotelling, conceived of most political competitions in terms of single-peaked preferences in such spaces.[3] Hotelling sought to derive generalized conclusions about political competition by analogy with one form of economic competition. His economic model analyzed the decision of where to place stores in a market. Hotelling's market was made up of consumers living along a single street. In the simplest cases, the consumers were assumed to live with uniform density along the entire street. The economic model, developed for the location of stores, indicated where the store should locate so as to attract the most customers. From this he drew the potential analogy between the location of stores and the policy positions adopted by politicians. The politician's task was the selection of a policy position to attract a majority of the voters.

Hotelling's major result was a derivation that the department-store competitors will cluster in the middle of the market (i.e. around the median customer). In his derivation, Hotelling assumed that the products offered by the two competitors were essentially the same and were offered at the same price. Thus, the decision of a consumer to patronize one store rather than another turned only upon the cost of travel to the store. Hotelling posited that travel costs increased with distance. From these assumptions, he was able to conclude that two competitors attempting to maximize their share of the market would attempt to locate at the center of the uniformly populated street. Each then would attract half of the consumers and would have no incentive to move. The store just to the left of the center would attract all consumers on the left half of the continuum. The store on the right would attract the consumers on the right. Were either to move off the center, the other would relocate next to the first, but on the side toward the center and capture more than 50% of the market.

Generalizing the notion of distance was the next step for Hotelling:

> Distance, as we have used it for illustration, is only a figurative term for a great congeries of qualities. Instead of sellers of an identical commodity separated geographically we might have considered two competing cider merchants side by side, one selling a sweeter liquid than the other. If the consumers of cider be thought of as varying by infinitesimal degrees in the sourness they desire, we have much the same situation as before. The measure of sourness now replaces distance, while instead of transportation costs there are the degrees of disutility resulting from a consumer getting cider more or less different from what he wants. The foregoing considerations apply, particularly the conclusion that competing sellers tend to become too much alike.[4]

[3]Harold Hotelling, "Stability in Competition," *The Economic Journal*, **39**, 1929, pp. 41–57. Reprinted in George J. Stigler and Kenneth E. Boulding, *Readings in Price Theory*, Chicago: Irwin, 1952, pp. 467–485. All page references are to the Stigler volume.
[4]Hotelling, *op. cit.* p. 481.

The application of these conclusions to the arenas of political competition is virtually self-suggesting. The competition of political parties is, after all, much like that of cider-merchants, one of product differentiation and not of geographical competition. Hotelling notes the analogy as follows:

> So general is this tendency that it appears in the most diverse fields of competitive activity, even quite apart from what is called economic life. In politics it is strikingly exemplified. The competition for votes between the Republican and Democratic parties does not lead to a clear drawing of issues, an adoption of two strongly contrasted positions between which the voter may choose. Instead, each party strives to make its platform as much like the other's as possible. Any radical departure would lose many votes, even though it might lead to stronger condemnation of the party by some who would vote for it anyhow. Each candidate "pussy-foots," replies ambiguously to questions, refuses to take a definite stand in any controversy for fear of losing votes. Real differences, if they ever exist, fade gradually with time though the issues may be as important as ever.[5]

This analogy to a two party democratic competition is, on first blush, appealing. Implicitly, parties take the place of stores, the voters are the consumers, a single spectrum of issue positions replaces locations in the market, and a voter's optimal issue position on the issue spectrum takes the place of his spatial location. Analogous to the cost of transportation, a voter's valuation of a party's issue-position is assumed to fall off with increasing distance from the voter's ideal position. With these elements, the application to political competition can be made (cf. Black's theorem) and the conclusion follows that in attempting to attract as many voters as possible, parties will converge to the middle of a single dimensional ideological spectrum. Political competitors thus come to be ideologically indistinguishable.[6]

However intuitively appealing such a conclusion regarding ideological competition might be, a closer analysis of its theoretical assumptions shows that it is overly simplified. Even Hotelling saw this:

> The reasoning, of course, requires modification when applied to the varied conditions of actual life. Our example might have been more complicated. . . . Instead of a linear market, we might suppose the buyers spread out on a plane. . . . The number of dimensions of our picture is increased to three or more when we represent geometrically such characters as sweetness of cider, and instead of transportation cost consider more generally the decrement in utility resulting from the actual commodity being in a different place and

[5]Hotelling, *op. cit.* p. 482.
[6]A number of political analysts have pursued the spatial model of Hotelling. Perhaps the most straightforward and well-known use of Hotelling is contained in Anthony Downs, *An Economic Theory of Democracy*, New York: Harper and Row, 1957. He introduces nonuniform distributions of voters along the single dimension. A two-dimensional generalization of Hotelling-Downs can be found in Gordon Tullock, *Toward a Mathematics of Politics*, Ann Arbor, Michigan: University of Michigan, 1967. Further developments of spatial assumptions have been spurred by the works of Peter Ordeshook and Melvin Hinic. These are nicely summarized and presented in Riker and Ordeshook, *op. cit.*, Chaps. 11 and 12.

condition than the buyer would prefer[7]. . . . The problem of the two merchants on a linear market might be varied by supposing that each consumer buys an amount of the commodity in question which depends on the [distance he is located from the merchants] . . . With elastic demand the observations we have made on the solution will still for the most part be qualitatively true; but the tendency for *B* to establish his business excessively close to *A* will be less marked.[8]

This last complication was formalized and again applied to politics in an article by Arthur Smithies in 1941.[9] He notes the failure of Hotelling's argument in its predictions of political phenomena:

> The purpose of this paper is to take some further steps in the direction of generalizing the theory of spatial competition. The very fact that Professor Harold Hotelling's pioneer article explained so successfully the close similarity of the Republican and Democratic platforms in 1928 indicates that something more was needed in 1936. It was probably true to say in 1928 that by moving to the center of electoral opinion neither party risked losing its peripheral support. The situation at the present time requires no elaboration; suffice it to say that neither party feels itself free to compete with the other for the undecided vote at the center, in full confidence that it will retain its support from the extremes of political opinion.[10]

Smithies followed up Hotelling's suggestion that if consumers must bear transportation costs as part of their purchase price, each consumer's level of purchase would be affected by his distance from the store. Thus, in locating their stores, managers have to consider the potential loss of business from more distant customers. Managers would thus have an incentive to refrain from converging to the center. According to Smithies, political parties encounter similar incentives. If two parties resemble one another too closely, they run the risk of alienating potential supporters on the extremes of the continuum. These individuals would fail to vote if the parties were too much alike.

But there is another reason for convergence to be limited. Incentives to vote or contribute to a preferred party in a two-way contest is *not* a function of the distance of the party from one's own optimal position. Rather, (as seen in Chaps. 3 and 5) the incentive is a function of the *distance between the parties.* Therefore, unlike merchants, politicians have reason not to attempt to resemble one another completely.

But even with this caveat, the conclusions regarding competition taking place over a single-issue dimension seem sound. For in such cases political competition can be shown to lead to a stable winning platform: a

[7]The generalization of the argument to more than a single dimension is crucial politically, and has some inherent difficulties of which Hotelling was not aware. These include the lack of equilibrium location points, as is discussed in the next section of this chapter.

[8]Hotelling, *op. cit.* p. 482–484.

[9]Smithies, "Optimum Location in Spatial Competition," *The Journal of Political Economy,* XLIX, 1941, pp. 423–439. Reprinted in Stigler and Boulding, *op. cit.,* pp. 485–501. Page references are to the Stigler and Boulding volume.

[10]Smithies, *op. cit.,* p. 485.

Condorcet winner. Politicians have a (limited) tendency to choose positions near the median optima. Such a model may well predict and explain the behavior in 'simple' political contests such as school-board budget fights and park-improvement projects. But in general elections, political competitions are seldom fought on the basis of a single issue. And these more complex electoral situations often will resist analysis using this model.

III. SHORTCOMINGS OF THE SPATIAL ANALOGUE

In the words of Donald Stokes: ". . . most spatial interpretations of party competition have a very poor fit with the evidence about how large-scale electorates and political leaders actually respond to politics."[11] Using survey data of voters' preferences and behavior in France and Finland, Philip Converse has concluded that a unidimensional model is inadequate if one is attempting to represent single-peaked preferences of individuals over parties.[12] He found that a multidimensional model of the competitive arena between the parties was needed to fit the data satisfactorily. In Finland, he required three dimensions to explain the party preferences of the voters. He identified one as a "standard" ideological dimension (a "left-right dimension"), another as an urban-rural dimension, and the third as a dimension defying his or our simple description. With these three dimensions, he was able to describe individual preferences as single peaked.[13] The multidimensional interpretation of single-peaked preferences is as follows: Each voter has a most preferred point in this three-dimensional space and his preferences fall off as one moves away from that point in any direction. Along any straight line, a point closer to the optimum is always preferred to a point farther away.

Now multidimensionality, per se, would not create any difficulties with our analysis, if, as Converse seems to assume implicitly, we can still expect that single peakedness leads to a Condorcet winner. Unfortunately, this isn't the case. Duncan Black has shown that in more than a single dimension, "the conditions which must be satisfied before there can be any majority motion (i.e. a Condorcet winner) are highly restrictive."[14] In general, then, a multidimensional competitive arena will involve cyclic preferences. Since Black's demonstration various scholars have attempted to prove that the

[11]Donald E. Stokes, "Spatial Models of Party Competition," in Angus Campbell *et al.*, *Elections and the Political Order*, New York: Wiley, 1966, p. 161.

[12]Philip E. Converse, "The Problem of Party Distances in Models of Voting Change," in *The Electoral Process*, M. Kent Jennings and L. Harmon Ziegler, ed., Englewood Cliffs, New Jersey: Prentice-Hall, 1966, pp. 175–207.

[13]See Brian M. Barry, *Sociologists, Economists, and Democracy*, London: Collier-Macmillan, 1970, pp. 136–142 for a critique of the Converse analysis as well as a broader critique of the entire question of dimensions in models of party competition.

[14]Duncan Black, *Theory of Committees*, p. 138. The proof, which is not difficult, is contained on pp. 131–138. The proof requires the use of indifference curve analysis as well as notions of contract lines. Since these are not part of the assumed background of the reader, the proof is a subject beyond the scope of this volume. But the assumption required to generate a Condorcet winner is so restrictive as to appear—at least to us—almost never to hold in the real world.

cycles will tend to be limited to rather special "subspaces" rather than cover the entire area. For example, imagine that it could be shown that although cyclic group preference would occur, the cycle could be restricted to the region around and close to the median voter's optimal preference point in both dimensions. Then the finding that cycles occur would not carry much normative weight, even if it might be of interest to us in predicting the outcome of any electoral battle.[15]

Donald Stokes constructs a more fundamental attack on the analogy of political space to physical space in markets (i.e. the location of stores).[16] Stokes argues that the issue space considered in the political analogue of Hotelling's model is "subjective" and "unstable" and hence quite different from the "main street" that served as the reality for the original model of spatial competition between two merchants. Stokes notes that the analogy would be jeopardized if there were a lack of consensus by voters of the issue positions taken by the politicians. That is, distance may not be intersubjectively meaningful: two individuals whom a researcher may indicate as having the same policy preferences, may, in fact, disagree as to which of the parties is closest to them. Similarly, politicians may not agree on the locations of voters in the issue space. Whether or not the undeniably subjective character of the issue space requires an abandonment of the spatial model is uncertain at this time. However, preliminary findings indicate that there is a good deal of intersubjective consensus regarding "closeness" of, and orderings of, parties to and from a given position.[17]

While multidimensional competitions fail to yield an equilibrium, and hence produce no Condorcet winner, a nonspatial approach to the problem of democratic decision making may prove to generate a determinate result. To consider this we next analyze two types of political decisions without using spatial constructs: (a) distributional questions, and (b) multiple issue situations where voters disagree about the relative importance of the issues to be decided upon by the group. In each case, we ask whether or not voting results in a determinate group choice. Furthermore, if there are indeterminate results we will examine the relative size of the subset of possible outcomes that may be included in the cycle.

IV. DISTRIBUTIONAL ISSUES

If multidimensional electoral competitions lead to preference cycles and all the vagaries attendant with such cycles,[18] one partial solution could lie in considering the issues "one at a time." It may be thought that since such

---

[15]This is because the policy outcomes would not vary greatly, all tending to be in the same region. This is the thrust of the argument by Gerald H. Kraemer, "A Dynamical Model of Political Equilibrium," Cowles Discussion Paper No. 396, New Haven, Connecticut: Yale University Press, 1975. Also see Tullock, *op. cit.*, Chap. 3.

[16]Stokes, *op. cit.*, pp. 168–176.

[17]Preliminary analogues of political spaces to other subjective spatial notions are discussed in Converse, *op. cit.*, pp. 182–184.

[18]The reader may wish to refer back to Chap. 1 where some of the arbitrariness associated with cycles was discussed. These and other aspects of cyclic choice will be discussed again in later sections of this chapter.

a process would lead to decisions that encompassed single issues, it would lead to Condorcet winners. Indeed, one can prove that:

> *if there is a Condorcet winner, considering issues "one at a time" will insure that it is the outcome to the majoritarian rules used in parliamentary bodies and committees.*[19]

But we still must ascertain how often we can expect Condorcet winners. To shed light on this question, let us analyze a class of issues which is prevalent in politics: distributional issues. Consider the use of democratic (majoritarian) procedures to decide a distributional question. Since de Tocqueville, sociologists and political scientists have conjectured that the adoption of democratic rules leads to (and protects) an egalitarian distribution of wealth.[20]

Let us consider how this conclusion stands up to close theoretical scrutiny. Imagine the problem attendant upon a simple distributional question: the division of $100 among three individuals' where the distributional plan must win a vote of a majority (i.e. two) of the votes. Is an egalitarian division a Condorcet winner in this simple case? Are de Tocqueville, Lipset, and others correct? If not, is there *any* Condorcet winner? Call the three voters i, j, k, and their shares in any distributional proposals, v_i, v_j, and v_k. Then can we construct a distributional proposal which defeats (by majority vote) the egalitarian proposal $v_i = v_j = v_k = 33 \frac{1}{3}$? Assuming that each voter is motivated primarily by his or her own share of the $100, the egalitarian solution can be beaten if we take the proceeds of any one of the individuals and redistribute them to the other two. In other words, i and j would both prefer dividing the $100 among themselves (50–50) and leaving nothing for k. The egalitarian solution is not a Condorcet winner. But the distributional plan that beats it is also unstable. For consider how an impoverished k would prefer any distributional scheme that could give him a share, no matter how meager! For example, i could grant k a share of the spoils (e.g. $v_k = 5$) and hold the rest for himself ($v_i = 95$). Both i and k would prefer this to the previous winner. It would defeat the previous 50–50 split between i and j. But any such plan is in turn defeated by the original egalitarian system. In summary:

	v_i	v_j	v_k	
	$33\frac{1}{3}$	$33\frac{1}{3}$	$33\frac{1}{3}$	is beaten
by	50	50	0	by the votes of i and j
is beaten by	95	0	5	by the votes of j and k
is beaten by	$33\frac{1}{3}$	$33\frac{1}{3}$	$33\frac{1}{3}$	by the votes of j and k.

[19]Joseph B. Kadane, "On Division of the Question," *Public Choice*, XIII, Fall, 1972, pp. 47–54.

[20]See for example, such works as Seymour Lipset, *Political Man*, New York: Doubleday, 1960 especially Chap. 2; Gerhard Lenski, *Power and Privilege: A Theory of Social Stratification*, New York: McGraw-Hill, 1966; Phillips Cutright, "Inequality: A Cross National Analysis," *American Sociological Review*, XXXII, No. 4, August 1967, pp. 562–578; and Anthony Downs, *op. cit.* Chap. 10, and p. 297.

The result is an absence of a Condorcet winner and the existence of a voting cycle. Moreover the result does not depend upon the number of individuals, nor the amount of money. A majoritarian decision rule does not lead to a particular distributional scheme. Rather: *Distributional issues always involve group preference cycles in majoritarian democracies.* This theorem is only one of the major results discovered by Benjamin Ward[21] in his analysis of the relationship between majority rule and distributions. This is a conclusion that is very far indeed from the conjectures of de Toqueville *et al.*

But not only do group preferences cycle in distributional issues, but the range of outcomes included in the preference cycles is enormous. As can be seen from the example, there is no exclusion of "relatively inegalitarian" results from the preference cycle. Results which were part of the constructed cycle include egalitarian schemes, equal shares for the positive gainers (50, 50, 0), and extremely concentrated wealth distributions such as (95, 0, 5). Indeed, *none of the logically possible outcomes can be excluded from the democratically chosen outcome except distributions giving all the wealth to a single voter.* This surprising theorem, proven in general by Ward, is not even restricted to include only those distributions which are Pareto optimal (i.e. those which do not waste some of the wealth).[22]

The alert reader may have already seen that there is a relationship between distributional questions and multidimensionality. After all, doesn't each individual (at least in the argument here) care *only* for his or her particular share of the spoils? If so, this would mean that each individual evaluates the proposal along a unique dimension: how big is *my* share and indifference to the shares of everyone else. In such a case, there is extreme multidimensionality in at least two senses: first, there are as many dimensions as there are issues; second, each actor only cares about one of the dimensions, and yet the dimensions are in direct conflict with one another. Clearly, the first aspect of the multidimensionality can be relaxed without altering our results. After all, instead of three individuals, we could have had three (homogenous) groups fighting to divide the spoils among themselves. Each group could have been a set of individuals who had agreed to try to increase the share of the proceeds for the group. Clearly, in such a situation, regardless of the actual number of voters, we would still have a cycle, even though there would be many more voters than dimensions. Thus, it appears that the extremely competitive nature of the situation[23] leads to the cycles. What happens in less extreme cases? To answer this, let us consider situa-

[21]Benjamin Ward, "Majority Rule and Allocation," *Journal of Conflict Resolution,* Vol. 5, No. 4, 1960, pp. 380–89.

[22]An article by K. Hamada, "A Simple Majority Rule on the Distribution of Income," *Journal of Economic Theory,* Vol. 5, pp. 243–264, shows that by assuming that the issue is raised regarding income to differing classes (no individual being named) the results may, sometimes, not involve cycles. This article contains a number of other interesting findings for the serious student.

[23]What marks a situation as extremely competitive is the characteristic that the preferences of the actors are inverses of one another. This is clearly the case on a purely distributional issue: the more one person gets, the less there is for others. Such situations have become known as "zero sum" in accordance with their classification according to the theory of games. See Luce and Raiffa, *op. cit.,* pp. 59–63 for an introductory depiction of such situations.

tions where the voters are broken into numerous groups, the members of any one group having similar preferences. Further, assume that unlike the pure distributional question (all for me, to hell with the others), each voter has preferences regarding all aspects of the final outcome (not only his own share), although not all aspects are of equal importance.

V. VOTE TRADING AND COALITIONS OF MINORITIES

An Illustration: Two-Sided Issues

Imagine two parties competing in an election in which the voters are concerned with three issues, each of which has two sides.[24] In order to imbue the example with some empirical referent, let us give the issues some substance. Let Issue One be whether or not Blacks and Chicanos should be afforded more civil rights. Issue Two can be the question of whether or not legislation allowing closed (or compulsory union) shops should be passed. Let Issue Three be the question of the extension or nonextension of price supports to farmers. The problem facing party strategists is the construction of a winning platform in which they take one of the sides on each of the issues. In each case let the Y position on the issue represent the pro minority position. Thus, for example a party platform such as YNY would consist of positions pro Black and Chicano civil rights, anti-union organization, and pro farm price supports. Suppose that the voters are composed of four disjoint (i.e. nonoverlapping) groups: 15 percent are Blacks and Chicanos; 30 percent are union members; 10 percent are farmers; and the remaining 45 percent are unaffiliated with any other groups. These may be construed as three minority groups and a residuum of others.

Assume each minority group stands alone in their preference for a policy favorable to their group. Only Blacks and Chicanos are for civil rights; only labor union members are for union shops; and only farmers are for price supports. But in addition to their standing alone on their "pet" issues, let us assume that each group feels more intensely about "their" issue than they do about the other issues combined. In other words, let them be so concerned about getting their way on their "bread and butter" issue that they would prefer winning on it and losing on the other issues to winning on the other issues and losing on their most important issue. Clearly this condition on their preferences is not as strong as the restriction on the condition of the three voters or groups in the distributional question. In that case the *only* aspect of the platform of concern to each group was how much *they* got. In this case each group is more concerned about their own issue than all others but they are concerned about the other issues as well.

[24]The analysis in the next paragraphs is developed more fully in Joe A. Oppenheimer, "Some Political Implications of 'Vote Trading and the voting Paradox: A Proof of Logical Equivalence'" *American Political Science Review*, LXIX, No. 3, Sept. 1975, pp. 963–966. For a published proof of the conclusions regarding two-sided issues, see Peter Bernholz, "Logrolling, Arrow Paradox, and Cyclic Majorities, *Public Choice*, XVI, Summer, 1973, pp. 87–102. A less self-conscious argument in much the same spirit can be found in Downs, *op. cit.*, pp. 55–60 and 64–69.

What sort of platform, then, should a party attempting to gain a majority of the votes put together in order to attract a winning coalition of voters?

The problem is depicted in Table 6–1. There we refer to a pro minority position on any issue as Y and a con position as N. The preferences of the members of the groups are set out in the table. From a glance at the table, the ideal platform for each group can be identified. Blacks and Chicanos prefer a platform of YNN; union members prefer NYN; farmers want NNY; and the unaffiliated desire NNN. Clearly, on each issue, an overwhelming majority prefers the N position to the Y position. Thus, 85 percent prefer N on civil rights, 70 percent prefer N on union shops, and 90 percent prefer N on price supports. Thus the one platform that, on the face of it, would appear to be a potential Condorcet winner is the one that takes the N position on all three issues, i.e., the NNN platform.

But a moment's reflection shows that the NNN platform can be beaten by the YYY position. In a contest between those two platforms, the Blacks and Chicanos would prefer the latter, since they get their way on their most important issue in that case, and similarly the union members prefer YYY to NNN as do the farmers. Only the unaffiliated prefer NNN. Thus in a contest between those two platforms, YYY would defeat NNN by 55 percent to 45 percent. The YYY platform—consisting of all minority positions—wins by attracting the support of a coalition of minorities.

Therefore, the NNN platform is *not* a Condorcet winner. But a little more reflection reveals that the YYY platform also fails as a Condorcet winner. The YYY platform can be defeated by any platform except NNN. For example, consider a NNY platform. In a contest between YYY and NNY the unaffiliated and the farmers prefer the latter to the former, and they constitute a majority of 55 percent. Only labor and ethnics support YYY. In turn, the NNY platform (and all platforms that can defeat YYY) can be shown to fail as a Condorcet winner. They all would lose in a contest with the minorities platform NNN. Consider a contest between NNY and NNN: the only question at issue is farm-price supports. A majority of 90 percent (all but the farmers) prefer N on that issue and so prefer NNN to NNY.

We have come full circle: a platform of NNN can be defeated by YYY which in turn can be defeated by NNY which is vulnerable to NNN. Group preferences, as represented by majority vote, cycle over these platforms and

Table 6–1   An Example of Two-Party Competition With Three Issues-Coalitions of Minorities

	Policy Preferences		
	Issue One Civil Rights	Issue Two Union Shops	Issue Three Price Supports
Blacks & Chicanos 15%	Y	N	N
Union Members 30%	N	Y	N
Farmers 10%	N	N	Y
Unaffiliated 45%	N	N	N

none is a Condorcet winner. Indeed, one could lay out the results of all possible pairwise contests in this situation and show that each platform is neither a Condorcet winner nor a sure loser. In this example voting cycles are the rule and every platform is a member of some cycle. Figure 6–2 sets out in schematic form the various cycles that are possible. Notice that any platform whatsoever could win by majority vote if it faced the "right" opponent. Various coalitions of different minorities are potential winners.

It follows immediately from this brief example that it is impossible to describe two-party electoral competition of this type in terms of competition along an ideological continuum that is single peaked. As noted above, if electoral competition takes place over a single-peaked continuum, majority vote yields a winner and precludes the possibility of cyclical majorities. In this example, cyclical majorities are possible, as we have seen. Therefore, it is impossible to rank the voters along an ideological dimension so that their preferences are single peaked. Hence, whenever issues make possible a winning platform consisting of coalitions of minorities, it is impossible to analyze political competition as having a unique and stable solution. Thus, the major reason for employing the spatial analogue (its ability to facilitate the identification of a solution) is missing.

The General Characterization of Coalitions of Minorities

The reader may believe that this cycling of group preferences follows only as a result of an idiosyncracy of the example constructed by the authors. Unfortunately for democratic theory, it is possible to identify some rather

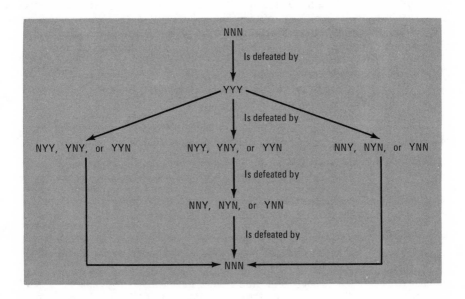

Figure 6–2   Cycles involving coalitions of minorities

general conditions under which one can construct coalitions of minorities and, hence, cyclic majorities.

If one restricts oneself to two-sided issues of any number, then the following distribution of preferences over the issues is enough to permit the construction of a coalition of minorities and hence a voting cycle in a majority vote situation:[25]

1. Over 50 percent of the voters find themselves in a minority on one or more of the issues. (i.e. they find that they support the side that only a minority favor on that issue.)
2. Those who find themselves favoring the minority side on some issue, who also feel more strongly about their minority position than about the positions on the other issues (on which they are on the majority sides) constitute over 50 percent of the electorate.

Put more simply, over 50 percent of the voters are in a minority position on some issue and feel more strongly about that issue than they do about all others combined.

Clearly our example has these characteristics, and it is possible to construct a general proof that the possibility of a coalition of minorities in such a situation implies preferences that support a voters' paradox.[26] As in the example, the set of all minority positions could defeat the platform consisting of all of the majority positions, since a majority feel more strongly about their minority position than they do about their majority position. Thus more than 50 percent would be willing to take a loss on their less important issues in order to guarantee themselves victory on their more passionately held issues. But in turn this platform of minority positions could be beaten by a platform that took some minority positions and some majority positions. Such a platform would be designed to appeal to enough minorities to give it more than 50 percent of the vote. Any such platform could, in turn, be defeated by a platform consisting of all majority positions on the issues.

[25]This result follows if one assumes that coalition formation is costless and subject to no "restraints". Since both of these assumptions are unrealistic in many contexts their relaxation has been of central concern in recent research in this area. See John Ferejohn, "Sour Notes on the Theory of Vote Trading," *Social Science Working Paper No. 41*, California Institute of Technology, Pasadena, California, June 1974 and Thomas Schwartz, Collective Choice, *Separation of Issues and Vote Trading*, Pittsburgh, Pa., Feb. 1975, mimeo. Both conclude that the results are more complex when these conditions are relaxed. A recent theorem, however, raises questions regarding the general need for a restrictive assumption on the costs of vote trading. See David H. Koehler and James M. Enelow, "Vote Trading in Context: An Analysis of Cooperative and Non-cooperative Strategic Voting," paper given at the meeting of the Public Choice Society, Roanoke, Va., April, 1976.

[26]Here it is assumed that the issues in question are independent. By that we mean that individuals' preferred positions on each issue are independent of what position is adopted on other issues. In other words the issues do not interact. This condition may be violated empirically quite often—but it does not shift the thrust of our argument. It only complicates it. See, for example, N. Miller, "Logrolling, Vote Trading, and the Paradox of Voting: Some Theoretical Comments." Paper given at Public Choice Meetings, Roanoke, Virginia, April, 1976.

And as intimated above, the result can be extended beyond two-sided issues. In a contest involving n issues upon each of which m different policy positions are possible, if a successful coalition of minorities is possible then a voting cycle is supported by the preferences of the voters, in a majority-vote situation.[27] And finally, by generalizing the voting procedure to require special majorities for victory, we can identify a variety of situations involving cycles.[28]

The Minimum Empirical Domain of Coalitions of Minorities

We have briefly characterized the situations under which coalitions of minorities capable of supporting cyclical majorities can occur. What is the likelihood that any of these theoretically possible situations occur in the world of political reality? A definitive discussion of this question would require a great deal of careful empirical research of a sort not yet performed.[29] Yet some of the characteristics of coalitions of minorities and references to some generalizations about politics can be used to argue that there are a number of empirical situations in which it is reasonable to expect the preferences of groups of individuals to support a coalition of minorities and hence a voting cycle.

The core of the argument turns on the question of intensities of preferences over different issues. If different groups of people have different intensities of preference over different issues, then one of the conditions identified above as leading to a coalition of minorities can be satisfied. Anthony Downs has discussed the question of variations of intensities of preferences. He also noted that modern societies involve substantial divisions of labor, and each such division potentially generates a number of strongly held minority issues.[30] These economic issues can form the basis of a coalition of minorities. As noted in Chap. 5, the price received by farmers for their crops seemed to have a major impact on their vote in the Presidential election of 1956. It is unlikely that this factor was as important for other voters in the society. But there we identified other issues that might form the components of a coalition of minorities. The voting patterns of American Jews were tied to the positions of the Democrats and Republicans on events in Germany in the 1930's and 1940's. The changed voting patterns of Blacks was attributed to the welfare programs of the depression

[27]The generalization to multisided issues was first done by Peter Bernholz, "Logrolling, Arrow-Paradox and Decision Rules: A Generalization," *KYKLOS*, 27 (fasc. 1, 1974) pp. 49–62.

[28]See Bernholz, *op. cit.*, and Joe A. Oppenheimer, "Relating Coalitions of Minorities to the Voters' Paradox or Putting the Fly in the Democratic Pie," a paper delivered at the annual meeting of the South West Political Science Association, San Antonio, Texas, March 30–April 1, 1972.

[29]But see William H. Riker, "The Paradox of Voting and Congressional Rules For Voting on Amendments," *American Political Science Review*, Vol. 25, 6/58, pp. 349–366, and John C. Blydenberg, "The Closed Rule and the Paradox of Voting," *Journal of Politics*, Vol. 33, No. 1, 1971, pp. 57–71 and Terry Sullivan, "Voter's Paradox and Logrolling: An Initial Framework for Committee Behavior on Appropriations." *Public Choice, XXV, Spring 1976, pp. 31–45.*

[30]Downs, *op. cit.*, pp. 255–256.

period, and differences in the Democratic and Republican response to these programs. The time honored practice of ethnically balancing tickets in ethnically diffuse constituencies can be explained in terms of an attempt to construct a coalition of minorities. The reactions of old-age pensioners to differences between the Republicans and Democrats on questions of social security and medicare in the 1964 election was another example of an issue that mobilized a minority of strong sentiments. We could continue cataloging minority issues which appear in the electoral arena almost indefinitely. But this brief discussion need only assert that the conditions which support a coalition of minorities are prevalent in a variety of electoral situations. As long as this is established, the consequences of elections with underlying voting cycles must be analyzed more carefully.

Vote Trading and Logrolling

Elections are not the only potential arena for preferences supporting coalitions of minorities. Legislatures and legislative committees often deal with issues on which only minorities feel passionate concern. The incidence of legislative logrolling and vote trading stands as testimony to the existence of a variety of such issues. Most policy decisions involve distributional aspects which favor minorities of some sort and so might support cycles.[31] Price support legislation for different commodities, tax legislation giving special advantages to particular groups, tariff legislation doing the same, rivers and harbors bills, and public works bills of all sorts are all areas in which minority groups can and do band together to pass bills that are coalitions of minority positions.

Two examples of such situations are given by Donald R. Matthews. One example discusses vote trading in the 1956 debate on acreage allotments for burley tobacco:

> Mr. Langer [North Dakota]: We don't raise any tobacco in North Dakota, but we are interested in the tobacco situation in Kentucky, and I hope the Senator will support us in securing assistance for the wheat growers in our State.
>
> Mr. Clement [Kentucky]: I think the Senator will find that my support will be 100 percent.[32]

The other example is a discussion by Senator Douglas of Illinois of the manner in which public works appropriations bills are put together:

> . . . This bill is built up out of whole system of mutual accomodations in which the favors are widely distributed, with the implicit promise that no one will kick over the applecart; that if Senators do not object to the bill as a whole, they will "get theirs." It is a process, if I may use an inelegant expression, of mutual backscratching and mutual logrolling.
>
> Any member who tries to buck the system is only confronted with an impossible amount of work in trying to ascertain the relative merits of a given project;

[31]Gordon Tullock discusses a theoretical model of such situations in "A Simple Logrolling Model," *American Economic Review*, 6, 1970, pp. 419–426.

[32] *U.S. Senators and Their World*, New York, Vintage Books, 1960, pp. 99–100.

and any member who does ascertain them, and who feels convinced that he is correct, is unable to get an individual project turned down because the senators from the State in which the project is located and thus is benefiting, naturally will oppose any objection to the project; and the other members of the Senate will feel that they must support the Senators in question, because if they do not do so, similar appropriations for their own States at some time likely will be called into question.[33]

What is the general relationship between "logrolling," "vote trading," and "coalitions of minorities?" What situations involving "vote trading" involve the cyclic characteristics of coalitions of minorities? These sorts of questions are, of course, partly definitional. However, in keeping with common usage, we can note that vote trading entails that one individual (i) decides not to vote his "preference on some issue because some other(s) (j) decide not to vote his preference(s) on some other issue(s)."[34] This switch is accomplished in a manner such that although i loses from his switch (when considered alone), he gains from j's and similarly, j, who loses from his switch, gains from i's.[35] Since both parties would clearly be "losers" if they acted in isolation from one another, vote-trading "requires that voters communicate and form agreements to adopt a particular" joint strategy.[36]

Now it should be clear that the developing of a coalition of minorities need not involve "vote trading" of an explicit sort. But this is because there is an implicit "logrolling" of issues in any electoral process. That is, the election will reflect simultaneous positions on a number of issues. Casting a vote for an individual, rather than for each of his or her issue positions separately, means that the issues are implicitly amalgamated in his or her platform. If we allow for a strategic combining of the issues, each of which might be unpackaged and handled separately, then the vote trades underlying the coalition of minorities are explicitly identifiable: as in the tobacco and wheat trade illustrated above. However, not all vote trades need be of the sort that we have depicted as underlying logrolls and coalitions of minorities. Indeed, we can characterize the sorts of vote trades underlying logrolls and coalitions of minorities as those which are supported by a majority of the voters.[37] That is, a majority of the individuals must prefer the outcome resulting from the trade to that which would have occurred

---

[33] *Ibid.*, p. 100.

[34] Note that if the issues aren't binary, the trade need not involve different issues.

[35] This definition is in keeping with the usage developed in the recent vote trading literature spawned by William H. Riker and Stephen J. Brams, "The Paradox of Vote Trading," *American Political Science Review* LXVII, No. 4, Dec., 1973, pp. 1235–1248 (c.f. p. 1238).

[36] David H. Koehler and James M. Enelow, *op. cit.*, p. 18.

[37] This is a somewhat more restrictive definition than is necessary. The more general formulation requires the notion of decisive coalition, which stems from Robin Farquharson, *Theory of Voting, op. cit.*, New Haven Yale University Press, 1969. For the derivation of the existence of stable outcomes with vote trades, see Thomas Schwartz, "Collective Choice, Separation of Issues, and Vote Trading." *American Political Science Review*, forthcoming. Further theorems are deducible from Schwartz' general formulation of the problem by a more thorough integration of the analysis with game theoretic concepts borrowed from Farquharson, c.f. Koehler and Enelow, *op. cit.*

without a trade. But this means that logrolling, which is the explicit vote trading across issues to constitute a majority out of a set of minorities, will involve all the characteristics of coalitions of minorities, as we depicted them. In sum, there is likely to be a fairly wide empirical incidence of preferences which are cyclic, and therefore, we can examine the implications of cyclic preferences in a variety of contexts.

Political Consequences of Logrolling and Coalitions of Minorities Situations

Having identified theoretical and empirical characteristics of coalitions of minorities, we can now evaluate the importance of this phenomenon for democratic politics. Our first major conclusion has to do with the utility of spatial analysis. The major product of spatial analysis is the identification of a stable equilibrium outcome in the policy space. If there is no such outcome, and if we cannot describe a region toward which the policy will move as a result of the competitive struggle, then there is no obvious utility in employing the spatial analogue. Our analysis indicates that there are severe limitations in the general use of spatial models to analyze democratic politics.

For example, when Downs analyzes party conflict using the distribution of voters along a single ideological continuum, he implicitly assumes that there are no coalitions of minorities.[38] Despite the intuitive appeal of analyzing party competition as requiring shifts "to the left" or "to the right" to win, the coalition of minorities argument shows this to be logically faulty. To the extent that party competition involves coalitions of minorities (and hence an absence of a "Condorcet winner") party competition won't dictate a movement toward an ideological median. Indeed, since coalitions of minorities invariably involve potential voting cycles, and hence no unique equilibrium, it is incompatible with one-dimensional analysis with single-peaked preferences. This is *not* to say that a majority of voters may not agree that one party "is further to the left" than the other party. However, when coalitions of minorities are possible, the parties' positions cannot be neatly *aggregated* into left-right packages *in a manner reflecting the preferences of the voters.* Although the notion of an ideological dimension may still have numerous uses, it clearly cannot help in the identification of a competitive equilibrium. Thus, for strategic vote-getting purposes, there may be no underlying continuum. If there is no continuum, there is no "center." There are only a variety of possible coalitional positions, any of which might win depending upon the strategic choice of platform by one's opponents.

Moreover, when winning coalitions are coalitions of minorities, it is unreasonable to expect most voters to agree on a well developed ideology. Imputations of "irrationality" to voters who fail to articulate consistent ideologies or to identify them in party actions are misdirected. Irrationality should be attributed, if at all, to those social scientists who insist in imposing a consistent unidimensional standard where none exists empirically.[39]

---

[38]Downs, *op. cit.*, Chap. 8.

[39]Philip Converse, "The Nature of Belief Systems in Mass Publics," in *Ideology and Discontent*, D. E. Apter, ed., New York: Free Press, 1964, pp. 206–261.

The absence of a Condorcet winner has another consequence that can be useful in understanding the dynamics of party competition. *In a coalitions of minorities situation, one party may win an election in a given year on a given platform and lose the following election on the same platform without any shift in the preferences of the voters.* This follows from the observation that any platform can be beaten by the appropriate strategic choice of the opposition. Thus, the rotation of parties in office on the basis of shifts in their programs need not signify anything about changes in voters' sentiment. A democracy with many minority groups may go through an extended period of changes in government in which policy outputs vary from programs catering to all minorities in the society, to programs representing the will of the majority on all programs. The policy reversals could be accomplished in the absence of any shifts in voters' preferences.

Moreover, the particular paths chosen through the possible cycles will have profound impacts on the various groups in the political arena. Referring back to Figure 6–2, we can compare the relative fates of the minority groups in two possible cycles. Comparing the relative fates of Blacks and Chicanos in two cycles is instructive of the possible variance in outcomes implied by voting cycles. Recall that the first entry in a platform represents the position of the candidate (or party) on civil rights for Blacks and Chicanos. A "Y" in that position is a pro-minority stance on Issue One. If competition proceeds through the extreme right hand path (YYY to YNN to NNN to YYY) with candidates alternating in office and acting on their platforms, the Blacks and Chicanos get their preferred position Y on their most important issue ⅔ of the time. If however, the competition proceeds through another possible cycle (YYY to NYY to NNY to NNN to YYY) then the same group gets its way only ¼ of the time. Similar conclusions can clearly be drawn about each of the other minorities.

The political competitors intent on putting together platforms designed to win have some degree of freedom in their choices of which cycles to choose in the absence of a Condorcet winner. In the absence of additional behavioral assumptions, there is no way of indicating which of the possible paths they will choose and which groups will consequently be advantaged and disadvantaged. Only if we add additional behavioral assumptions such as vote maximization, profit maximization, etc. as motivational substance for the political leaders, are other conclusions derivable.[40]

The existence of these equally win-producing options for politicians leads to another consequence of note. Constituents who are aware of the numerous alternatives from which politicians can choose their coalitions and programs do well to ask what motivates the politician (other than a desire to win). This is needed to predict which strategies will be chosen. Politicos who choose to back a group's policy merely to win a contest may well abandon the group on the morrow. Thus, some indication of strong loyalty to the ideals, goals, programs, etc. of the group should be very

---

[40]Some consequences of vote-maximization are discussed by Gerald Kramer, *op. cit.* Consequences of profit maximization can be found in Norman Frohlich, Joe Oppenheimer and Oran R. Young, *Political Leadership and Collective Goods,* Princeton: Princeton University Press, 1971, and Frohlich and Oppenheimer, "The Carrot and the Stick: Optimal Program Mixes for Entrepreneurial Political Leaders," *Public Choice,* XIX, (Fall, 1974), pp. 43–63.

important in the political valuation of the leader by his potential supporters. Thus, especially for groups without sufficient resources to buy their future membership in a winning coalition, the candidate's personal values, altruism, and actual group membership will be among the most important considerations in their evaluation of political leaders. Indeed, it may well be that herein lies the most important difference between self-interested and altruistic political leaders. Leaders who choose their policy positions with only instrumental valuations of these positions for personal gain cannot be trusted to stick with the policy, even if doing so would not jeopardize political victory. Thus, tangible evidence of a leader's personal valuation of the group's goals is often an important aspect of an individual's evaluative process regarding political competitors.

Of course, many of these conclusions regarding elections have implications for those other arenas of voting: committees and legislatures. In logrolling situations involving coalitions of minorities, the ultimate outcome is potentially as arbitrary as it is in the electoral arena. In this context, the later a particular platform enters into the voting, the more likely it is to win. Thus, control of the agenda becomes critical in such situations. In the U.S., this power, which in many cases is the power to decide the ultimate outcome of the legislative voting procedure, is vested in the leadership in Congress and Congressional Committees.[41] It explains the disproportionately large role played by the leadership in legislation.

A particular example of the impact of this consideration is the set of rules established by the House Ways and Means Committee to make the underlying voting cycle manageable. Since a particular tax break favorable to a minority could be defeated by a majority in a vote of the entire House, some procedure is needed to allow for catering to special-interest groups. The procedure is the so-called "Gag Rule." A tax program is set up by the process of logrolling and vote trading within the Committee. Various interests of minorities with the mobilizable resources necessary to influence members or a member of the Committee are aggregated into a program. Then the whole tax program is sent to the House for debate and vote *with the provision that the program as a whole be voted on and that no amendment can be made to the bill without the UNANIMOUS consent of the Committee.* This proviso is essential for the passing of the special-interest sections of the bill. Without it, each of the special provisions could be voted on separately, or amended out, by a majority vote, and then blocs of them could be added on again, and the process could go on indefinitely. The unanimity requirement insures that an issue of major importance to even one member of the Committee cannot be separated from the bill and defeated. The package as a whole is constructed so that enough members get their way on an issue of major importance to them that they prefer the passage of the bill with special favors for others rather than the defeat of the bill. The particular minorities

[41]Charles R. Plott and Michael E. Levine, "On Using the Agenda to Influence Group Decisions: Theory, Experiments, and an Application," *Social Science Working Paper, No. 66,* Pasadena: California Institute of Technology, Nov. 1974, examine analogous manipulative possibilities.

who get into the bill are determined by the Chairperson. (He or she controls the agenda in the Committee and the votes of the Committee members. No wonder chairpersons are considered powerful by observers of politics in the House.)[42]

But the coalition of minorities argument can shed light not only on the nature of political competition in the electoral and legislative arenas, but also on the nature of issues that are excluded from these arenas. If one posits that the rewards that politicians receive are in large measure associated with and derived from victory in electoral competitions, then they can be assumed to be highly motivated to win. Thus in selecting policy platforms upon which to run, they can be expected to avoid sure losing positions. Some issues and platforms not involving coalitions of minorities can be seen to be sure losers. The characteristics of such programs are relatively easy to sketch.

We will call issues which can guarantee loss to the imprudent politician *passionate majority issues*. The defining characteristic of a passionate majority issue is that people on the majority side of the issue value the sum of the issues on which they are in a minority less than they do their majority issue. In other words, they feel more strongly about that issue than they do about the combination of all issues in which they are a minority. Thus, they won't trade their vote for the majority side on this (most important issue) for victory on the other issues. It follows that any politician who takes a minority stand on a passionate majority issue would lose to an opponent who took the majority stand on that issue. Thus, on any passionate majority issue, no win oriented politician should be expected to espouse the minority position. Therefore, issues which a majority feel most strongly about would never enter into the electoral arena because political contenders would never find it worthwhile taking opposing positions on those issues. If there are passionate majority issues, then the democratic system would appear to guarantee the majority side on them without their ever entering into the electoral arena.

---

[42]Terry Sullivan, *op. cit.* Contrast this conclusion with that of Jimmy Breslin, who never quite gets beyond the notion of power as illusion:

Power is an illusion.

Illusion. Mirrors and blue smoke, beautiful blue smoke rolling over the surface of highly polished mirrors, first a thin veil of blue smoke, then a thick cloud that suddenly dissolves into wisps of blue smoke, the mirrors catching it all, bouncing it back and forth. If somebody tells you how to look, there can be seen in the smoke great, magnificent shapes, castles and kingdoms, and maybe they can be yours. All this becomes particularly dynamic when the person telling you where to look knows how to adjust the mirrors, ... [A]nd all the time keeping those watching transfixed, hoping, believing himself. Believing perhaps more than anybody else in the room. And at the same time knowing that what he is believing in is mirrors and blue smoke.

This is the game called politics and power as it is played in the Legion Halls and Elks Clubs and church basements and political clubhouses throughout the country, throughout the world, while men try to please and calm others in order to maintain and improve a public career.

Breslin, *op. cit.*, pp. 31–32.

This is the optimistic side of the coalition of minorities argument. *Passionate majority issues are protected by the democratic process, per se, without the necessity of constant contention in the electoral arena.* The dark side of the argument reappears when we ask: "If passionate majority issues aren't consciously chosen to differentiate parties, then which kind of issues are?" The answer to that is: "Only issues over which it is possible to construct coalitions of minorities."

Thus, voting cycles are possible for the issues that enter into the electoral arena, and the policy outputs over the issues counted in the electoral arena are subject to the sort of arbitrariness discussed above even if there are issues which can be characterized as passionate majority issues.

As a consequence of this analysis, we can derive some conclusions regarding the differential impact of two incentives for voters to turn out in elections. The issues that a majority of the voters care about most are provided for by the democratic system *per se.* Thus, the greatest benefit is provided the majority not by the issues decided in the arena, but by the issues that are provided because of the arena. We would expect that potential voters would experience a greater incentive to vote in order to protect and preserve the *system* that guarantees them the preferred position on the passionate majority issues than to make a difference in the decision regarding the issues contested in the electoral arena. By the same token, we would expect those individuals who find themselves to be in a minority position on passionate majority issues to experience a greater incentive to vote from the issues contested in the arena than from the system-support aspect of the act of voting. This follows because individuals who feel strongly about their minority position on a passionate majority issue will not be greatly supportive of the system that locks out this issue from the campaign.[43]

VI. SOME NORMATIVE CONCLUSIONS

Arrow's General Impossibility Theorem, discussed in Chap. 2, raised the possibility that a majority rule democracy might, on some occasions, be subject to arbitrary decisions. Proponents of democracy, of which we are two, might hope that this possibility would be limited in empirical scope. Unfortunately the arguments in this chapter indicate that cyclical group preferences may be all too common in a number of democratic arenas. If parties and candidates take stands on distributive issues, the set of possible positions will be such that voting cycles would occur over them. And since most, if not all, policy questions involve some distributive aspects, such potential cycling is likely to be widespread. Moreover it is a clear fact of life that people have different intensities of preferences over different issues. To the extent that this is a precondition for the construction of coalitions of

[43]Note that the structure of the political system may mitigate these effects. Thus, for example, centralized and disciplined parties running on "national platforms" will exacerbate the effects. On the other hand loosely knit parties, with candidates running on locally engineered coalitions, can recognize local passionate majorities, and hence increase system-support motivations.

minorities, and hence voting cycles, the spectre of cycles is raised even in non-distributive issues. We must reluctantly conclude that cycles occur more often in democratic societies than is usually presumed. A simple probabilistic model would also tend to underestimate the incidence of cycles, as would a projection based on actually observed cycles. The latter holds because often a voting cycle may exist but the control of the agenda cuts off the cyclic process before the cycle is completed. The former holds because the probabilistic models developed to date do not permit combining issues through vote swapping.[44] Attendant upon these cycles are the arbitrariness of various democratic decisions and the special privilege which accrues to those who control the agenda setting process. Our attention is drawn to the power that inheres in agenda setting functions. If cycles occur often, then the power to determine the order of nomination procedures, votes on amendments, forms of referenda, etc., is often the power to determine the outcome. Moreover, if cycles are pervasive, they undercut the legitimacy of claims that a majority vote in support of a candidate and his platform constitute an unequivocal mandate, i.e., "the will of the majority." To understand who gets what when and how in a democracy requires the careful analysis of the agenda-setting process.

Despite the importance of some of these conclusions, one might object that they have been derived in a relatively rarified theoretical atmosphere in which too many simplifying assumptions have been made for the sake of theoretical neatness and exposition. Indeed, in general, we have assumed that potential voters and politicians have pretty good knowledge regarding one another's strongest preferences and that voters need not worry about a candidate's capability to implement his or her programs. We have argued as if there were only one governmental office and one constituency. Furthermore, we have argued as if all constituent groups of coalitions of minorities have uniform preferences. Strictly speaking, the arguments advanced in this chapter cannot be maintained if one or more of these assumptions is found not to hold in an empirical case to be analyzed. Yet the results are striking and at least call for further study. What happens when the systems violate the simplifying assumptions? This is researchable and should be answered. After all, any theoretical explanation ultimately will require a careful working out of the diverse models in all their complexity and a comparison of each of their predictions with the appropriate empirical phenomena.

Prior to the development of these more detailed models, one can question the value of presenting the simplified model. We feel that it is useful to identify the simpler theoretical core that underlies the general problem to be explored. Thus, the examination of the cyclic basis of logrolling, etc. underlies a number of problems in democratic theory and practice. The analysis of these phenomena hopefully sheds light on the dynamics of some party competitions, and the dynamics of committee politics when the committee has a strong (agenda-setting) chairperson.

---

[44]A solid, if somewhat sceptical review of probabilistic projections of vote cycles can be found in Sen, *Collective Choice and Social Welfare*, (Holden Day: San Francisco, 1970), pp. 163–166.

VII. FOR FURTHER READING

The literature relevant to the analysis of this chapter is growing rapidly. It is hard for the average reader to find papers before publication (as cited in many of the footnotes). But some of the work (especially regarding the spatial and distributional models) has been available for a number of years. A worthwhile survey of the spatial literature can be found in Riker and Ordeshook's, *An Introduction to Positive Political Theory* (Englewood Cliffs: Prentice-Hall, 1973). But Ordeshook also published a less technical review of the literature "The Spatial Theory of Elections: A Review and a Critique," in *Party Identification and Beyond,* Ian Rudge, et al. ed. (London: Wiley, 1976), pp. 285–314.

On the subject of distribution and voting, there is, once again, a quickly developing literature. Aside from the works indicated in the footnotes, the reader may wish to examine such works as Amartya K. Sen, *On Economic Inequality* (New York: Norton, 1973)—which is a wide ranging, if technical, introduction to the subject as well as Donald E. Campbell, "Income Distribution Under Majority Rule and Alternative Taxation Criteria," *Public Choice,* XXII, Summer, 1975, 23–36, which identifies ethical criteria, which if imposed upon the shape of a taxation program, lead to equilibria.

Finally, on the relationship between the preferences of one's constituents and one's platforms, there is a wide ranging literature including many of the articles and books cited above. But the reader should consider examining Benjamin Bental and Uri Ben-Zion, "Political Contribution and Policy —Some Extensions," *Public Choice,* XXIV Winter, 1975, 1–12; Uri Ben-Zion and Zeev Eytan, "On Money, Votes and Policy in a Democratic Society," *Public Choice,* XVII (Spring 1974), 1–10; as well as the empirical data contained in Warren E. Miller and Donald E. Stokes, "Constituency Influence in Congress," *American Political Science Review,* Vol. 57 (no. 1), March, 1963.

INDEX